FARMHOUSE KITCHEN
Microwave Cook Book

A fourth book based on the Independent Television series presented by Grace Mulligan. This collection of *Farmhouse Kitchen* recipes has been adapted for the microwave cooker by Marie Emmerson.

Edited by Mary Watts

YORKSHIRE TELEVISION

First published in Great Britain 1986 by

YORKSHIRE TELEVISION ENTERPRISES LTD
Television House, 32 Bedford Row,
London WC1R 4HE
© Yorkshire Television Enterprises Ltd., 1986

FARMHOUSE KITCHEN is a Trade Mark of Yorkshire Television Ltd

ISBN 0 946064 16

*Acknowledgments: front cover illustration courtesy of Fine Arts Photographs,
London;
back cover photograph from Yorkshire Television, by Alan Harbour.*

Text illustrations: Mary Evans Picture Library

Reprinted 1986 (twice)
Reprinted 1987
Reprinted 1988 (three times)

Printed in Great Britain by
Richard Clay Ltd, Bungay, Suffolk

CONTENTS

FOREWORD

by Grace Mulligan

At last I'm having fun using my microwave. Despite my experience as a cook, I took a long time to get used to this shining new box in the kitchen. There were times when I was very tempted to use it just as a pie-warmer and de-froster. I had plenty of disasters. I tried cauliflower florets for the specified four minutes. I went on cooking and prodding them for a further ten minutes but they never did become tender. Bendy carrots just stayed bendy and got more and more tough. All this because I didn't think I needed to read the instructions. Microwaves work on moisture and my vegetables were not perfectly fresh. The lesson I learned the hard way is that really fresh vegetables bring superb results. Speedy microwave cooking retains natural moisture, preserves colour and texture and is therefore much healthier. I find that the flavour of my freshly-picked herbs, chopped and microwaved with a little butter for about 30 seconds, gives me a stunning, simple sauce for vegetables, fish or chops.

My microwave is endlessly useful for many of the preparations needed for everyday cooking. It softens chopped onions like magic, cooks fruits perfectly in hardly any water and brings butter to room temperature in just a few seconds. Soup is so easy, there is little steam and certainly no worry about it catching or burning. All sauces, from an ordinary white one to an elaborate Hollandaise, are simplicity itself. You even get quite used to all that whisking and stirring which seems so much more frequent than in traditional sauce-making, because the total time taken is so short.

Generally speaking, food which in ordinary cooking needs water (boiling, steaming, poaching) will do well in a microwave. Food needing dry heat, like pastry, pancakes and Yorkshire puddings, are not suitable for microwave cooking. Similarly, you cannot fry food in deep oil or fat. Our baking section is quite small and we have included only the recipes which work well. I still haven't found a good Victoria Sponge recipe, but I understand some packet mixes give a good result. Meat cookery is very successful too, making roasting, braising, and casseroling both time-saving and economical. Cooking fresh fish gives superb results. For quick proof of this, here is a simple fish recipe.

Ingredients 2 thin fillets of fish (haddock or sole)
25 g/l oz butter
2 tablespoons lemon juice
1 tablespoon chopped fresh parsley

Method   Put the butter, lemon juice and parsley in a shallow dish. Microwave on full power for 30 seconds. Turn the two pieces of raw fish in this flavoured butter and lay them side-by-side. Cover and cook on full power for 4 minutes, or until set and no longer 'glassy' (but very white).

I do hope you will enjoy our book, with all the recipes we have adapted along with the advice and cooking tips. You will very soon be able to look at your microwave cooker with pleasure and know that it earns its place in your kitchen and that you've mastered yet another skill.

My best wishes to you. Do write to us if you would like to. Your letters are always welcome and, who knows, perhaps you can tell us something useful about microwave cooking.

Presenter of the 'Farmhouse Kitchen' television programmes.

Why not do these recipes the first day you have your cooker, especially if you are expected to prove that the thing works and that the investment is going to be fruitful! They are easy and rewarding.

A Baked Potato

Ingredient One raw potato – about 175g/6 ozs

Method   Wash and dry the potato and prick all over with a skewer. Stand the potato on a piece of paper towel. Microwave, uncovered, on full power for 6 minutes or until the potato is soft. (Add a further 3 minutes to the cooking time for 2 potatoes.) Split and top with a little salt and pepper and perhaps some grated cheese and chutney.

Filling variations Cream cheese and chives; garlic butter; baked beans.

Bacon & Scrambled Eggs

Ingredients 6 thin rashers of rindless streaky bacon
              2 large beaten eggs
              15 g/$\frac{1}{2}$ oz butter
              4 to 5 tablespoons of milk
              Salt and pepper

Method   Lay the rashers side by side on one piece of paper towel and cover them with another piece. Microwave on full power for 4 minutes. Set aside and keep warm while you do the eggs.

             Put all the ingredients into a deep bowl. Whisk well and cook on full power for 2 minutes. Whisk again and cook for a further 2 minutes, or until the eggs are softly-set but still runny in the centre. Remove from the cooker, season and serve on hot buttered toast with the bacon.

ACKNOWLEDGMENTS

This selection of recipes covers a wide variety of dishes which you may already know if you have used our earlier **Farmhouse Kitchen** books. They have been chosen not just to give you ready-made conversions of proven recipes, but also to show how, with some experience, it becomes possible to adapt your own.

The people whose names appear throughout this book originally gave us their recipes for **Farmhouse Kitchen** programmes and publications that were devoted to traditional, conventionally-cooked everyday dishes. They have all kindly agreed to having these recipes converted for microwave cookers.

The selection of suitable recipes and the adaptation has been skillfully done by Marie Emmerson. Well-known, not only because of her life-long association with Jenny Webb of the Electricity Council, but because she has taken a professional and personal interest in microwave cooking since 1975. As an authority in the field she lectures frequently, and has contributed for many years to 'Freezer Family' and 'The Food Magazine'. Two more of her books will be published in 1986.

As is our custom with all **Farmhouse Kitchen** publications, these recipe conversions have been thoroughly tested, mostly by Grace Mulligan and myself, but also by a valued team who have been associated with the television programmes since they began fourteen years ago. I am indebted once again to Sybil Norcott, Anne Wallace, Biddy Clayton and Bunty Johnson.

A relative newcomer to the programmes has been Joan Tyers, who was amongst the first of the experts to encourage Grace Mulligan and **Farmhouse Kitchen** viewers in the use of the microwave cooker. Joan has contributed a helpful list of hints and tips to this book.

The endless typing, checking and correcting which accompanies the preparation of cookery books has been in the hands of Amanda Hart and Joyce Town.

To all these valued contributors I owe and extend grateful thanks and admiration.

Mary Watts
Autumn 1985

Yorkshire Television's **Farmhouse Kitchen** series is produced and directed by Mary and Graham Watts.

INTRODUCTION

by Marie Emmerson

WHAT YOU NEED TO KNOW

Before you start to experiment with your microwave cooker, there are several things that you *need* to know to help you get the best from it and so add to the pleasure of this new form of cooking.

Wattage Output

The time taken to cook any dish will depend upon the wattage output of your cooker. So, check the wattage from either your cooker manufacturer's book, the rating plate fitted probably to the back of the cooker, or from the shop where you bought it. This information is essential to you when using recipes from any microwave book or magazine or from instructions on food packets.

All our recipes have been tested on a cooker with a 650 to 700 watt output. If your cooker has a lower watt output than this then **you may have to add a few extra minutes** to the total cooking times. As a guide: for a **500 watt output cooker add about 20 seconds for every minute,** for a **600 watt output cooker add about 15 seconds for every minute.**

Controls

Each cooker manufacturer uses different terminology and power levels for the control dial: there might be numbers such as 1 to 10, words, symbols, or percentage figures. To simplify our recipes we have, with only one or two exceptions, used just two settings: Full Power (100%) and Defrost (30%). So check for these positions on your cooker. You can, of course, use any other setting but we suggest that you may prefer to try those when you become more familiar with your cooker.

Containers/Materials

Your own microwave cooker handbook should give you full guidance as to the best containers and types of material to use, but **the golden rule is never to use metal or metal decorated containers** as the microwaves reflect off metal and you could damage your cooker. Remember to **replace metal ties on roasting bags with elastic bands or string**, and if you use basketry, ensure that the basket is not held together by metal staples or wires. However, providing the manufacturer recommends it for your cooker, **small pieces of foil may be used to mask thin areas of food** – e.g., the tail of a fish – as this prevents them from overcooking. Be careful though not to let the foil touch the walls of the cooking cavity as this can cause arcing (flashes of blue light), which is not only off-putting but could cause pitting to the walls of the cooker. A further caution: **avoid using antique china and good lead crystal** as they may break or crack when

7

subjected to the heat of the food. Initially, you may not always need special microwave containers and you might find it more convenient to use your existing china and oven-to-table glass.

Later on, once you have worked out your particular needs, you may wish to choose microwave containers to suit your personal style. But **avoid using shapes with squared-off corners as overcooking in the corners can occur**. Rounded corners are better. Also, choose containers which will not allow the contents to boil over. For example, do not use a 1 pint (600 ml) jug for 1 pint (600 ml) of sauce. A $1\frac{3}{4}$ pint (1 litre) jug is the minimum size to use for this quantity of liquid.

To help you with our recipes we have tried to use the smallest number of containers, all of which are the oven-to-table, glass or Pyrex type. We chose these because most kitchens have them and the shapes are suitable. The following should cover most of your cooking requirements:

Large bowl	$4\frac{1}{2}$ to 5 pints	(2.75 litre)
Medium bowl	$3\frac{1}{2}$ pints	(2 litre)
Small bowl	2 pints	(1.2 litre)
Small jug	1 pint	(600 ml)
Large jug	$1\frac{3}{4}$ pints	(1 litre)

Quantities in Recipes

We do not recommend increasing the quantities of ingredients given in recipes in this book until you are quite experienced. There are several reasons for this. The cooking times would need to be increased, your containers may not be large enough to contain the extra quantities, and frequently it would be quicker and more economical to cook them by the conventional method. **The microwave cooker is a tremendous aid in the kitchen but you cannot expect good results if it is overloaded with food.**

Manufacturers Instructions

Although it may not be your favourite reading, it *is* worth taking some time to **read the instructions supplied by the manufacturer of your cooker** as they give lots of useful information. I have summarized much of what can be found in the books, but as there are over one hundred different microwave cookers on the market your own instructions should be referred to for precise information.

When Not In Use

The microwave cooker should not be operated without food or liquid in the cooking cavity. So, as a precaution (especially with inquisitive children around) leave a cup of water in the cooker when it is not in use. Most microwave cookers do have a protective device if they are operated when empty but if yours doesn't damage could occur.

WHAT YOU MAY WANT TO KNOW

How the Microwave Cooker Works

We all understand that when conventional heat is applied to food it cooks by conduction (e.g., frying an egg), by convection (e.g., baking a cake) and by radiation (e.g., grilling a steak). Microwave cooking can cause a little confusion to a new user because heat is not used, yet food can be thawed, re-heated or cooked. So, it is quite useful to appreciate how it actually works without having to learn the technicalities.

Microwaves are electro-magnetic waves, similar to those used for a television and radio. Just as a television needs a tube to give a picture, so a microwave cooker needs a magnetron to generate microwaves.

The microwaves usually enter the cooking cavity from the top and a slow paddle, fan or stirrer deflects them towards the metal walls to give an energy pattern.

All microwave cookers have at least two 'interlocks' so the microwave energy can only be generated when the door is closed and the appropriate controls are switched on. **As soon as any attempt is made to open the door the magnetron stops generating microwaves**. Microwaves cannot pass through metal because metal acts as a barrier – so they simply bounce off. They cannot pass through the door of the cooker as it has an inner lining of highly-engineered metal mesh to prevent this.

However, microwaves can pass through any other material, such as paper, china and glass. To the microwaves, such materials are invisible. As a result, **the container will only get hot from the heat of the food.**

But microwaves react differently to food. Food and liquid are moist and contain moisture molecules. **Microwaves are attracted to moisture**, and once food or liquid is placed in the cooking cavity, and the cooker is switched on to generate microwaves, they immediately concentrate their energy on the food.

This raises an interesting point if you are cooking or reheating something which contains both a solid food and liquid – e.g., a stew. The liquid will absorb energy more quickly than the meat. So if you only test the liquid, you could find that the meat is not hot enough, or even not cooked, when you serve it.

Cooking Procedures

When cooking conventionally you automatically treat the food in the best way in order to achieve the best result – by stirring, basting, turning over and re-arranging whenever required. The same applies to cooking in the microwave cooker. However, as it is such a new method of cooking we have given some guidance in our recipes to save you having to make the initial decision.

Stirring: Stir liquids to ensure even heating and, for example, to avoid lumps in sauces. Stirring other foods, such as vegetables, helps even cooking.

Turning over: Although not always necessary, large joints and birds will cook more evenly if turned over at least once during cooking.

Rearranging: As different models of microwave cookers may not have the same energy pattern, it is possible that some areas of solid foods – such as chops – will get more, or less, energy. So, by rearranging the food, usually halfway through cooking, you are likely to achieve an even result.

Turning round: Some foods, such as puddings, cannot be stirred, turned over or rearranged, but to contribute to an even rise and cooking you can give the container a half turn.

Standing time: If food is cooked for too long in a microwave cooker it tends to dehydrate and harden or, in the case of sauces, thicken. This is because the natural moisture has been given off in the form of steam – rather like a cake over-cooked in a conventional oven which ends up hard and unpalatable. To avoid this, **it is better to undercook rather than overcook** with many foods such as fish, meat and vegetables. Once you have removed and checked the food, extra cooking time can always be given. However, some foods can finish cooking by conduction, using the heat which has been generated within the food itself. So, **a standing time is recommended before serving. This is very important with large, thick foods such as joints and birds**. If you carved these immediately, or removed them from the cooker, they would be so undercooked that nobody would want to eat them!

Our recipes indicate if a standing time is required. If there isn't such an instruction, then it is usually either because the time taken to serve the food is in itself sufficient to constitute a standing time, or it has been allowed for in the cooking time – for example, when cooking a casserole on defrost (30%).

Arrangement of food: Generally, **there is less microwave energy in the centre of the cooking cavity** and this can be a useful thing to remember, especially when cooking small pieces of food of different shapes or density, like chops and broccoli. If you place the thinner ends of the chops, or the delicate 'flower' of the broccoli towards the centre of the cooking container, there is less likelihood of these parts overcooking and becoming tough.

You can use the same arrangement with fish fillets, but if there isn't enough space then tuck the thin end of the fillet underneath itself. By doing this you are increasing the thickness, and this should prevent overcooking. As the centre area receives less energy, it is better to arrange more evenly-shaped small foods, such as jacket potatoes, in a circle so that there isn't one in the centre. Also, leave a space between each so that all the potatoes can benefit from the maximum amount of microwave energy. Think of it like this: you don't squash food together in a conventional oven as you want to make sure that it obtains the maximum benefit from the circulating heat.

Covering food: It can be difficult to decide whether or not to cover foods, but it is very much like conventional cooking. For example, when boiling, steaming or stewing on a hob you use a cover. When making sauces, or scrambling eggs, you do not use a lid or cover. When baking in a conventional oven, a covering is not used. But when you roast food, the use of a cover depends upon your personal preference.

The same generally applies to microwave cooking. If you want the food to cook in, or retain, its own moisture, you cover it. If you want a 'dry' product, then you don't.

As with all cooking techniques, there are exceptions to this, but we have indicated in our recipes whether or not you need to use a cover.

The type of cover you use is entirely up to you. You could use a plate or a casserole lid; or cling-type film, which has to be pricked in several places to avoid a build-up of steam; or the types of film suitable for microwave cooking which do not have to be pricked. Just a tip: **when removing any cover, raise it from the side away from you to avoid the steam burning you.**

There may be times when you may wish to cover but still want a 'dry' result, especially if the food has a tendency to spit or splatter. In these instances, a piece of kitchen paper towel will do the trick.

WHAT CAN BE COOKED IN THE MICROWAVE COOKER

Some people claim that they can cook everything in a microwave cooker, but it normally depends upon individual food-buying and eating habits. For example, a super cake-maker is unlikely to use the microwave cooker, whereas a fish-eater is likely to use nothing else. The following points are for general guidance only. As always, the final decision will rest with you, the cook.

What Works Really Well

Cooking soups, fish, sauces, meat dishes made up of tender meat and poultry, fruit and vegetables. Gelatine dishes such as cold soufflés, mousse, etc. Making confectionery, jams and chutneys. Reheating most foods, other than pastry. Warming liquids, such as milk. Thawing frozen foods. Melting chocolate, fat and syrups.

What Works Fairly Well

Cooking tough cuts of meat, provided that a low enough power is available. Game and rabbit, to which the same is applicable. Some cakes, provided that you find the lack of texture and colour acceptable, and some biscuits developed for microwave cooking. 'Steamed' puddings, but these generally need eating immediately they are ready. Suet puddings, if you find the texture of the pastry acceptable. Shortcrust flan cases, if you don't require a good colour. Jacket potatoes, if the lack of a crisp skin is acceptable. Some bread doughs, but they turn out soft and colourless.

What Really Does Not Cook Well

Yorkshire puddings, choux pastry, roast vegetables (such as potatoes), hot soufflés, tarts and pies using raw pastry. Reheating foods already cooked in batter, and any other food which requires heat to 'set' the rise, brown the product or make it crisp.

What Should Never Be Cooked

Deep fat or shallow fat frying, as the temperature of the oil/fat cannot be closely controlled. 'Boiling' eggs in shells, as the pressure from the heated egg could cause the shells to break, and this could damage the cooker. This operation should only be carried out if the cooker manufacturer gives instructions for it.

WHY DID IT GO WRONG?

Like any form of cooking, the unexpected may happen when you use your microwave. Things can go wrong for one or more reasons. Naturally, it isn't possible to cover all eventualities, but the following are answers to the questions people most often ask.

Q Why does butter spit when being melted?
A Just like conventional cooking, it can be due to overheating or to the fact that the butter contains more water than usual (for example, if it has been frozen). It is a good idea to check frequently during melting or to remove it when it has partially melted and stir to finish the process.
Q Why is it that the same quantity and type of food, such as milk, sometimes heats more quickly than at other times?
A Remember, food at room temperature will heat more quickly than food from the refrigerator. Or, in the case of solid foods like vegetables, have they been cut smaller than on previous occasions? Or have you used a different type of container?
Q Why do pre-cooked pastry pies and tarts tend to have soggy pastry on reheating?
A Because microwaves are attracted to the moister parts, such as gravy or syrup, in the filling. This heats and boils, giving off steam which is absorbed by the pastry. This can sometimes be overcome if the product is removed when the pastry is warm to the touch rather than hot.
Q Why do cakes sometimes go hard on cooling?
A There may be several reasons. The specified egg size or liquid was not used, thus reducing the moisture content of the cake mixture. Or the container was larger than the one recommended, or the cake was cooked for too long.
Q When I use my own recipes I do not get my usual results, or they fail completely. Why?
A It is difficult to adapt recipes unless you have had a lot of experience. The easiest way is to follow another similar microwave recipe for guidance.
Q My suet puddings go hard on cooling. Why?
A This is a common occurrence because there is so little moisture in the pastry to begin with and, once cooled, the remaining moisture is given off in the form of steam causing the pastry to dehydrate and harden. See also a suggestion of Joan Tyers', page 113 (S for Suet puddings).

Q Why do apples or potatoes in their skins burst when I cook them?
A Because the 'flesh' cooks and gives off steam which cannot escape through the skin. Pressure builds up and eventually causes the skin to burst. This can be avoided by pricking the skins before cooking.
Q Why can't I cook vegetables to the very soft stage? The longer I cook them the tougher they get!
A Because vegetables are cooked in very little water and rely on their own moisture to cook. If cooked for too long they will dehydrate and toughen. If you prefer very soft vegetables then you should use the conventional cooking method in a saucepan on top of the stove.
Q Is a standing time really necessary?
A In many instances it is essential (see my notes on page 9).

REHEATING FOOD IN THE MICROWAVE COOKER

Reheating food is fast and efficient and, when correctly reheated, food will not get that sad, unpalatable look that can occur when you reheat on a conventional hob or in a conventional oven. However, like conventional reheating it is essential to ensure that foods are very hot, particularly in the case of meat, poultry and game, simply because **warm, half-heated foods can cause tummy upsets.**

Tips for Reheating
When reheating **slices of meat or poultry always spoon over some gravy or stock.** This will prevent the meat from heating too quickly and dehydrating.

To avoid loss of moisture, **cover most foods** with a lid, plate, or cling film (which has been pricked to allow steam to escape).

'Dry' foods, such as **cooked bread rolls and pastries,** should not be covered as this will only cause the moisture to return into the food and make it soggy. With these products, remove them when they are warm to the touch rather than hot, otherwise they will harden on cooling.

A meal on a plate will take about $3\frac{1}{2}$ to $4\frac{1}{2}$ minutes to reheat, but much will depend on what is on the plate, so it is worth checking it from time to time during the reheating process.

Should you want to reheat **more than one plated meal,** stacking rings made of plastics can be used. However, as more food is in the cooking cavity the reheating time will be longer. See Joan Tyers' suggestion on page 113 (R for Reheating).

Correct arrangement of food on the plate will help to achieve the best result. Thought should be given to the density and texture of the food. For example, slices of meat, creamed potatoes and peas. The potatoes are dense and take longer to heat than the meat or peas. So, rather than arranging them in a pile, flatten them so that they are not so thick. The peas will heat quickly as they are small, so these are best arranged in a pile rather than spread out, to make them deeper. As the meat is thin, cover it with gravy so it will not overheat and dehydrate.

THAWING FOOD

Food thaws very quickly in a microwave cooker compared with conventional thawing but, **once thawed, the food should be treated like all fresh foods and used at once.**

Many foods such as **hamburgers, sausages, fruit, vegetables and sauces, and also completed dishes,** can be thawed using the highest power setting, but thicker ones such as **joints of meat or poultry** thaw more evenly when you use the defrost (30%) setting.

A standing time is frequently suggested by food manufacturers and is particularly beneficial when you are thawing large joints of meat and poultry. This ensures that the food does not start to cook in those areas where the ice has thawed, and gives the remaining 'icy' area an opportunity to finish thawing naturally. We have given guidance in the various food chapters within this book but always check and follow the manufacturer's instructions where they are given in your microwave cooker handbook, or on food packages.

Defrost (30%) is the better setting to use with certain **cakes, pastries and breads;** for example, a cream gâteau, Danish pastry or loaf of bread.

Generally, foods are covered when thawing to keep as much 'warmth' within the food, but **it is better to leave dry products, such as cakes, breads and pastry, uncovered.** Place these on a piece of kitchen paper towel, which will help to absorb any moisture and prevent the base of the food getting soggy. These foods, like meat, should not be completely thawed but given a standing time to complete the process.

Other foods such as **sauces, soups, casseroles, stews, fruits and vegetables** thaw more quickly if you break them up gently with a fork during thawing. It is also helpful to choose a container which is large enough to avoid boiling over on reheating, yet of such a shape that it will keep the thawed liquid close to the frozen block. Where foods contain pieces of ice which are not a part of a sauce, the ice can be removed, as the microwave energy will simply be wasted on a part of the product which is not required.

Smaller, solid pieces of food such as **chops or larger joints** benefit from being rearranged or turned over during thawing. If overheating occurs during the process, use small pieces of foil secured by a wooded cocktail stick as protection but, as always, ensure that the foil does not touch the cooking cavity walls. **Tails of fish** can also be wrapped in foil for the same purpose.

Some foods such as **vegetables or meat and fish in sauce** can be thawed in a 'boil-in-the-bag', but it should be pricked or left open to avoid a build up of steam which could cause the bag to burst.

The arrangement of food for thawing follows the same principles as cooking, and this is covered on page 10.

Chapter 1

Soups and Starters

Some extra useful information, but not necessary for following the recipes.

Soups *are easy to make in the microwave cooker and there is never the problem of scorching which can spoil flavour. Generally, the high power setting is used, and the vegetables and meat are cooked prior to adding liquid. A large container should be used to avoid boiling over and a cover is advisable to avoid evaporation.*

Hot stock *is recommended as the microwave cooker takes a long time to heat liquid, and with such large quantities this is the fastest and most economical method. If you use cold stock there will be no appreciable saving of time and it would be better to make the soup in a saucepan on top of the stove.*

When thawing soups *it is wise to choose a container small enough to keep the thawed liquid close to the frozen block but large enough to cope with boiling over on heating. During thawing you can gently break up the mixture with a fork and stir it now and then to speed up the process. 1.1 litres/2 pints of soup will take about 20 minutes to thaw on full power.*

TO MAKE CHICKEN STOCK

A tip

Grace Mulligan suggests the stock will be richer if the bones are first baked until brown in a hot oven, Gas 7, 425°F, 220°C, for about 15 minutes before following the instructions given below.

Chicken carcass, trimmings from wings and legs and the giblets

1 small onion, quartered
1 small carrot, cut in pieces
A small piece of celery
1 bay leaf
6 peppercorns
1 litre/1¾ pints hot water

1. Put all ingredients in a large (2.75 litre/4½ to 5 pint) bowl. Cover and cook on full power for 10 minutes.
2. Reduce to defrost setting (30%) and cook for a further 15 minutes.
3. Allow to cool and then strain. If it is not to be used at once refrigerate or freeze.

Sybil Norcott
Irlam, Nr Manchester

A tip

Liquid heated in a tall, narrow container is likely to boil up and over even after removing from the microwave cooker. It is advisable to use a wider container. If a liquid should start to boil over, opening the door will stop it.

Bunty Johnson

HOT BEETROOT SOUP

This soup freezes well, but do this before yoghurt or soured cream is added. A liquidiser is needed.

Serves 6

450 g/1 lb raw beetroot, do not use old woody beetroot
450 g/1 lb potatoes
2 onions
50 g/2 oz butter or margarine
1.5 to 1.75 litres/2½ to 3 pints hot strong chicken stock
Salt
Freshly ground pepper
To garnish: yoghurt or soured cream

1. Peel and dice beetroot and potatoes. Peel and chop onions. Put them in a large 2.75 litre/4½ to 5 pint bowl.
2. Add butter or margarine. Cover and cook on full power for 15 minutes. Stir halfway through cooking. If the potatoes are waxy it may be necessary to cook for 3 minutes more.
3. Stir in the hot stock, do not cover. Bring to the boil.
4. Cool the soup and reduce it to a purée in liquidiser. Adjust seasoning.
5. Just before serving, bring soup to boiling point and serve with a swirl of yoghurt or soured cream in each bowl.

Grace Mulligan

CARROT SOUP

Serves 4

2 onions
1 clove of garlic
450 g/1 lb carrots
40 g/1½ oz butter
A pinch of salt
Pepper
1 dessertspoon coriander seeds
½ glass of sherry
450ml/¾ pint hot chicken stock
450ml/¾ pint milk
To garnish: chopped parsley

1. Peel and slice onions. Crush garlic. Put both into a large (2.75 litre/4½ to 5 pint) bowl. Add the butter.
2. Scrub carrots, slice thinly and add to bowl with salt and pepper, coriander seeds and sherry.
3. Cover and cook on full power for 10 minutes or until carrots are tender. Stir halfway through cooking.
4. Add the hot stock, bring to the boil, uncovered. Allow to cool.
5. Liquidise or sieve the soup, then strain into a clean jug or serving dish. Alternatively, using a food processor a less fine consistency is possible and you can better enjoy the flavours of the different ingredients.
6. Add milk when ready to serve. Reheat carefully on full power, but watch it to see that it only just comes to the boil. Adjust seasoning.
7. Sprinkle parsley in each bowl of soup.

Grace Mulligan

CREAM OF LEEK AND POTATO SOUP

Simple ingredients, but a superb soup.

Serves 4

4 medium-sized leeks
4 small potatoes
50g/2oz butter
150ml/¼ pint water
600ml/1 pint hot chicken stock
Salt and pepper
150ml/¼ pint thick cream

1. Wash and trim leeks and chop into small pieces, using both white and green parts. Peel potatoes and cut into small cubes.
2. Put leeks and potatoes into a large (2.75 litre/4½ to 5 pint) bowl.
3. Add butter and water. Cover and cook on full power for 20 minutes. Stir halfway through cooking. Take out 1 or 2 pieces of the deep green leek leaves for garnishing.
4. Add the hot stock, do not cover, cook on full power until boiling.
5. Put soup through a food processor, or a liquidiser or rub it through a sieve. Return it to the bowl or to a tureen. Season to taste with salt and pepper.
6. Stir in the cream, do not cover, reheat on full power, but do not boil. Finely shred the reserved pieces of leek and drop a little into each bowl when serving.

For a dinner party the soup can be prepared in advance up to and including paragraph 5. It will take about 10 minutes uncovered on full power to reheat from cold. Stir in the cream at the last minute, but do not let it boil again.

Mrs Eileen Trumper
Llanvair Kilgeddin, Gwent

A tip

Salt toughens and causes dehydration of meat and vegetables cooked by microwave. Always salt afterwards for vegetables or late in cooking for meat. Less salt is needed for vegetables cooked by microwave because their natural salts are retained as so little water is used.

Joan Tyers

SIMPLE ONION SOUP

Serves 4

4 large onions, about 675 g/1½ lb
40 g/1½ oz butter or margarine
900 ml/1½ pints hot, well-
flavoured chicken stock
Salt and pepper

1. Peel onions, slice very finely and put them in a large (2.75 litre/4½ to 5 pint) bowl.
2. Add the butter or margarine. Cover and cook for 12 minutes. Stir halfway through cooking. Check onions are cooked before going on to next stage.
3. Add heated stock, season to taste, return to microwave cooker and bring to the boil.

Mary Watts

CREAM OF TOMATO SOUP

Freezes well, but do so before milk or cream is added.

Serves 4

1 medium-sized carrot, scrubbed
1 onion, peeled
2 sticks of celery, washed
75 g/3 oz butter or margarine
A 400 g/14 oz tin of tomatoes
1 teaspoon sugar
600 ml/1 pint hot light stock
Salt and pepper
25 g/1 oz plain flour
1 tablespoon tomato paste or
purée
150 ml/¼ pint top-of-the-milk or
single cream
To garnish: chopped parsley

1. Slice carrot, onion and celery finely. Put them in a large (2.75 litre/ 4½ to 5 pint) bowl.
2. Add 40 g/1½ oz of the butter. Cover and cook on full power for 9 minutes. Stir halfway through cooking.
3. Add tomatoes with their juice, sugar, 300 ml/½ pint of the heated stock, salt and pepper to taste. Return to microwave cooker and bring to the boil.

4. Depending upon the consistency you like, either put the mixture through a food processor or put it through a liquidiser and then through a sieve to remove the tomato pips.
5. Put the remaining butter into a 600 ml/1 pint jug. Cook on full power uncovered for 1 minute. Stir in the flour and gradually blend in the remaining stock. Stir in the purée.
6. Cook uncovered for 3 minutes. Stir every minute to avoid lumps.
7. Now add this to the tomato mixture and stir in the milk or cream. Check seasoning. Heat to nearly boiling point, but do not actually boil or the soup may curdle.

Serve sprinkled with chopped parsley.

Dorothy Sleightholme

Smells. If you cannot remove a smell by wiping the cooker with a hot damp cloth and a spot of detergent: put a piece of lemon rind or a dash of lemon juice (bottled variety is suitable) into a small bowl with 300 ml/½ pint water and let it boil uncovered in the microwave cooker on full power for 1 to 2 minutes. Then wipe with a clean tea towel.

Joan Tyers

MINTY TOMATO SOUP

This is a refreshing soup, cooked by microwave the flavours and colours are distinct.

Serves 4

450 g/1 lb fresh ripe tomatoes, or a 400 g/14 oz tin
1 large onion
25 g/1 oz green pepper
25 g/1 oz butter, margarine or good bacon dripping
0.5 to 1 litre/1 to 1¾ pints hot chicken stock

Pinch of basil (optional)
1 bay leaf
Salt
Black pepper
½ teaspoon sugar (Barbados preferred)
1 dessertspoon chopped mint
1 tablespoon chopped parsley (optional)

1. If fresh tomatoes are used, peel them. To do this, put them in a bowl and cover with boiling water. Wait 30 seconds then pour off hot water and cover with cold. Wait half a minute and skins will be easy to remove. Chop up tomatoes finely.
2. Peel onion and chop finely.
3. Chop green pepper very small.
4. Put the onion, pepper and butter into a large (2.75 litre/4½ to 5 pint) bowl. Cover and cook on full power for 5 minutes. Stir halfway through cooking.
5. Add tomatoes, hot stock, basil and bay leaf. Cover and cook for 12 minutes.
6. Test seasoning, adding a very little salt if necessary, plenty of freshly-ground black pepper and the sugar.
7. Just before serving add chopped mint and parsley.

To make a meal of this soup add a handful of cooked brown rice, brown macaroni or fancy pasta when soup comes to the boil.

Mary Watts

AVOCADO AND SALMON MOUSSE

A liquidiser or food processor is useful.

Serves 4 to 6

225 g/8 oz tinned salmon
15 g/½ oz gelatine
6 tablespoons water
2 avocado pears
½ teaspoon salt
A dash of pepper
2 teaspoons anchovy essence
3 tablespoons single cream

18

2 or 3 drops of green food
colouring
2 egg-whites
To garnish: 1 stuffed green olive,
chopped fresh parsley

1. Drain salmon. Reserve juice.
Remove bones, skin and flake the flesh
finely.
2. Put the water in a small cup or
bowl. Cook on full power uncovered
for 30 to 45 seconds. Sprinkle over the
gelatine and stir until completely
dissolved.
3. Split, stone, skin and cut up the
avocados. Scrape as much pulp as
possible from skin as this will give the
mousse a deep green colour.
4. Liquidise the avocados, salt, pepper,
anchovy essence and salmon juice. Or,
if you do not have a liquidiser or food
processor, mash thoroughly and beat
until smooth.
5. Place in a large bowl, strain in the
dissolved gelatine. Stir in cream and
flaked salmon adding green colouring
if needed.
6. Whisk egg-whites until they will
stand up in peaks. Then fold into
salmon mixture.
7. Turn into a fish or ring mould
which has been rinsed in cold water,
and leave to set.
8. Turn out into a serving dish.
Garnish with the stuffed olive, for
eyes, and parsley.

This recipe would make excellent
individual ramekins too. Remember
that avocado discolours quickly so the
mousse should be eaten the day it is
made.

Grace Mulligan

See also Salmon Mousse, page 25

FRESH MUSSELS WITH PARSLEY

Serves 2

450 g/1 lb fresh mussels in the
shells*
15 g/½ oz butter

½ a large clove of garlic, crushed
1 dessertspoon parsley

**Mussels should be eaten the day
they are bought. If necessary store
overnight in a cool place, but not in
water.*

1. Wash and scrub mussels, pull off
the beards. Using the back of an old
knife, knock off any barnacles. Discard
any open mussels.
2. Put the mussels, butter, garlic and
parsley in a large (2.75 litre/4½ to 5
pint) bowl. Cover. Cook on full power
for 3½ minutes or until the mussel
shells open. Stir halfway through
cooking.
3. Serve immediately with crusty
French bread to mop up the delicious
soup.

Grace Mulligan

A tip

Cheese spread and pâté will spread
further in sandwiches or on toast if
heated on full power for only 5
seconds.

Grace Mulligan

LIVER PÂTÉ

Pâtés are spectacular in the
microwave because of the time saved
compared with conventional cooking.

For this you need a liquidiser or a food
processor.

Can be kept in refrigerator for a week
or in freezer for 6 weeks, but long
freezing is not suitable because garlic
flavour tends to get a bit strong.

*As a lunch or supper dish, enough
for 5 people. As a starter, 10
portions.*

Sauce

20 g/¾ oz butter
20 g/¾ oz flour
150 ml/¼ pint milk
Salt and pepper

Other ingredients

225 g/8oz chicken, calf or lamb's
 liver
15 g/½ oz butter
A clove of garlic, crushed
125 g/4oz fat bacon pieces
Half a sour apple, peeled, cored
 and sliced
4 anchovy fillets
1 egg
175 to 200 g/6 to 7 oz streaky
 bacon rashers
1 bay leaf

1. Start with the sauce. Put the butter in a 600 ml/1 pint jug. Cook uncovered on full power for 30 seconds or until melted. Stir in the flour.
2. Gradually blend in the milk. Cook uncovered for 2 minutes. Beat hard halfway through cooking to make sure sauce is smooth. Season with salt and pepper.
3. Trim skin and gristle from liver if necessary and cut into 2.5 cm/1 inch pieces. Put it into a medium-sized (2 litre/3½ pint) bowl.
4. Add the 15 g/½ oz butter. Cook covered on full power for 3 minutes.
5. Put it in liquidiser or food processor with garlic, bacon pieces, apple, anchovy, egg and sauce. Switch on and process till mixture is smooth. Season to taste with salt and pepper.
6. Line a microwave ring mould with streaky bacon.
7. Pour in liver mixture and arrange bay leaf in pieces on top. Cover closely with plastic wrap or cling film.
8. Cook on full power for 10 minutes.
9. Remove from microwave cooker. Press the pâté with a weight on top until it is cold.
10. Turn out on a plate and serve in slices with salad, Melba toast or hot toast and butter.

Anne Wallace
Stewarton, Ayrshire

A tip

Standing time. As a general rule of thumb, allow one third of the cooking time. All foods require it but the denser the food the longer it takes.

Joan Tyers

STUFFED RINGS OF RED AND GREEN PEPPERS

A very pretty and delicious dish. For this you need a liquidiser or food processor.

Serves 6 or more

2 small red peppers
2 small green peppers

Stuffing

This is a pâté of chicken livers which can be made in larger quantities to serve on its own. Can be frozen, but only for 1 or 2 weeks. Do not freeze in the peppers, which would be spoilt by freezing. Fill into flat dishes, smooth the surface and firm up in the fridge. Then pour on melted butter to seal the surface. (Butter can be melted in microwave.)

125 g/4 oz chicken livers
1 onion, finely-chopped
25 g/1 oz butter
1 tablespoon oil
A clove of garlic, finely-chopped
½ level teaspoon chopped fresh
 thyme, or ¼ level teaspoon dried
125 g/4 oz cream cheese
Salt and pepper
To serve: hot buttered toast

1. Cut a lid off each pepper with its stalk and hollow out by removing core, seeds and white membrane.
2. Prepare chicken livers by scraping out core and cutting away any part tinged with green. Chop, but not small.
3. Put the onion in a medium-sized (2

litre/3½ pint) bowl. Cover and cook on full power for 3 minutes.

4. Stir in the livers, butter, oil, garlic and thyme.

5. Cover and cook for 4 minutes. Stir halfway through cooking. Cool.

6. Put the mixture through a liquidiser or food processor until smooth.

7. Add cream cheese, salt and pepper. Continue processing until well combined and the texture is thick and smooth.

8. Fill this mixture into the hollowed-out peppers. Chill.

9. Just before serving, cut each stuffed pepper into 1 cm/½ inch rings and arrange prettily on individual plates.

Serve with hot buttered toast.

Grace Mulligan

Flat-headed Brittany Artichoke.

Chapter 2

Fish

Some extra useful information but not necessary for following the recipes.
Cooking fish in the microwave is very successful, and as little or no liquid is required the special flavour of fish can be enjoyed to the full. Generally, the container is covered to keep the moisture in, and the high power setting is used.

As a general rule of thumb, allow 3 to 4 minutes per 450 g/1 lb for thin pieces of fish such as fillets, and 5 to 10 minutes per 450 g/1 lb for steaks and whole fish. Standing time is about 5 to 10 minutes. Care should be taken not to overcook – the fish is cooked when the flesh easily flakes and is opaque.

Check your manufacturer's instructions for food arrangements but generally place the thinner ends of fish steaks to the centre of the container and tuck the thin ends of fillets under themselves. Whole fish can have small pieces of foil wrapped around the tails but make sure this does not touch the cooker walls.

Fish must never be fried in a microwave cooker because the temperature of oil and fat cannot be monitored.

Thawing: *If the fish is in sauce, choose a container small enough to keep the thawed sauce close to the fish. If pieces of fish are frozen together, gently separate them during the thawing process. Generally, the full power setting can be used and a cover will ensure there is little loss of moisture. Allow about 4 to 5 minutes per 450 g/1 lb and if possible give a standing time of about 5 minutes. The fish is thawed when no ice remains.*

See page 110 for Joan Tyers' tips on cooking fish from frozen.

SPANISH COD

A delicious dish for a special occasion. It also works well using fillets of coley. Skin them first.

For 4 people

4 cod steaks, allow 150 to 175 g/ 5 to 6 oz per person

Sauce

25 g/1 oz butter or good margarine
25 g/1 oz plain flour
150 ml/¼ pint white wine

150 ml/¼ pint water, liquid from cooking fish may be used
Pepper and salt

Topping

1 tablespoon chopped green pepper
50 g/2 oz chopped onion
1 tablespoon olive oil
50 g/2 oz sliced mushrooms
2 tomatoes, peeled, sliced and seeds removed
50 g/2 oz prawns
1 tablespoon chopped parsley
Pepper and salt

1. Place the cod steaks, with the thin ends to the centre, in a casserole dish. Cover and cook on full power for 4 minutes. Set aside covered.
2. For the sauce, put the butter in a 600 ml/1 pint jug. Cook uncovered on full power for 30 seconds or until melted.
3. Stir in the flour and gradually blend in the wine and 150 ml/¼ pint of the fish liquid or water. Cook uncovered for 4 minutes. Stir every minute to avoid lumps. Season with pepper and salt. Set aside covered.
4. For the topping, put into a small 1.2 litre/2 pint bowl the pepper, onion and oil. Cook covered on full power for 3 minutes or until peppers are soft.
5. Stir in the mushrooms, tomatoes, prawns, parsley, salt and pepper.
6. Lift the fish out of the casserole for a moment and pour in the sauce. Place the fish on top. Spread the topping over fish. Cook uncovered for 3 to 4 minutes or until hot.

Anne Wallace
Stewarton, Ayrshire

Shallow dishes are generally best for microwave cooking. Things will cook faster. Round rather than square, oval rather than rectangular. Food in corners tends to over-cook.

Joan Tyers

SMOKED HADDOCK IN SCALLOP SHELLS

Enough for 6 shells

Creamed potato

1 kg/2 lb potatoes
4 tablespoons milk
50 g/2 oz butter

Other ingredients
700 g/1½ lb smoked haddock

750 ml/1¼ pints milk
50 g/2 oz butter or margarine
50 g/2 oz flour
125 g/4 oz lightly-cooked green peas
75 g/3 oz grated cheese, Parmesan and Cheddar mixed
Pepper and salt

1. Prepare potatoes: peel and cut into 2 cm/¾ inch cubes. Put them in a large (2 litre/3½ pint) bowl with the milk and butter.
2. Cover and cook on full power for 10 to 11 minutes, then set aside covered for 3 minutes.
3. Place the fish in a shallow casserole dish. Cover and cook on full power for 6 minutes. Set aside covered.
4. Put the butter in a large (1 litre/1¾ pint) jug. Cook uncovered for 1 minute or until melted. Blend in the flour. Gradually add the milk. Cook for 6 minutes or until thick but stir after 2 minutes and then every minute to avoid lumps.
5. Stir in the peas, 50 g/2 oz of the cheese, pepper and salt – but remember the fish is salty.
6. Meanwhile, mash the potato and put it in a piping bag fitted with a large fluted nozzle.
7. Flake the haddock, removing skin and any bones.
8. Fold the haddock into the sauce and adjust the seasoning.
9. Pipe the potatoes as a border around the scallop shells.
10. Fill each shell with fish mixture. Sprinkle on the remaining cheese and brown under a preheated grill.
Can be reheated in the shells, but cover with cling film, prick it and heat on full power, 3 shells at a time, for 5 minutes or until hot.

Grace Mulligan

PILAFF OF SMOKED HADDOCK

Serves 4

350 g/12 oz smoked haddock
1 tablespoon oil
25 g/1 oz butter

1 onion, chopped
1 green pepper, chopped
175 g/6 oz brown rice
1 pint boiling chicken stock
1 teaspoon turmeric
2 tomatoes, skinned and
  chopped
Pepper
Chopped parsley

1. Trim fish, removing any skin and
bone. Cut it into bite-sized pieces.
2. Put the fish in a medium-sized
(2 litre/3½ pint) bowl. Cover and cook
on full power for 4 minutes. Stir
halfway through to ensure even
cooking. Set aside covered.
3. In a large (2.75 litre/4½ to 5 pint)
bowl put the oil, butter, onion and
green pepper. Cook covered for 3
minutes.
4. Stir in the rice, stock and turmeric.
Bring to the boil. Cover and cook for
20 to 25 minutes depending on the type
of brown rice you are using. Leave to
stand covered for 7 minutes.
5. Stir in the fish, tomatoes and
pepper. Cook uncovered for 3 to 4
minutes to heat.
6. Sprinkle liberally with chopped
parsley just before serving.

Anne Wallace
Stewarton, Ayrshire

MUSTARD HERRINGS

Serves 4

4 fresh herrings, prepared
  weight about 700 g/1½ lb
Salt and freshly-ground black
  pepper
25 g/1 oz butter
50 g/2 oz onion, finely-chopped

Mustard sauce

15 g/½ oz butter
15 g/½ oz flour
1 large teaspoon made English
  mustard
A pinch of sugar
4 tablespoons milk
150 to 300 ml/¼ to ½ pint water
40 g/1½ oz grated cheese

1. Scale, gut, wash and trim heads,
tails and fins from herrings. Cut each

one open from belly to tail. Press out
flat, skin side uppermost, and press
along backbone. Turn fish over and lift
out backbone from tail to head. Fold
back into the original shape.
2. Place the herrings in a shallow
casserole dish. Dot with 25 g/1 oz of
the butter. Cover and cook on full
power for 6 minutes. Re-arrange
halfway through cooking. Set aside
covered.
3. Put the onion into a 600 ml/1 pint
bowl. Cover and cook for 2 to 3
minutes. Set aside.
4. Now for the sauce. Put the butter
in a 1 litre/1¾ pint jug. Cover and cook
for one minute.
5. Mix in the flour. Gradually stir in
the mustard, sugar, fish juices from
casserole, milk and enough water to
make a fairly thin sauce. Cook
uncovered for 4 minutes. Stir every
minute to avoid lumps.
6. Beat in half of the cheese.
7. Scatter cooked onion over the
herrings. Pour sauce over. Sprinkle
with the rest of the cheese and brown
under a preheated grill.

Grace Mulligan

FRESH MACKEREL SPICED IN CIDER

Serves 6

6 small mackerel, filleted
1 medium-sized onion, sliced in
  rings
Wholewheat flour seasoned
  with salt and pepper
300 ml/½ pint apple juice,
  sparkling or still, or cider
½ level teaspoon pickling spice
2 bay leaves

1. To fillet the fish, follow
instructions in Portland-style
Mackerel.
2. Put onion rings in a bowl with 1
tablespoon of the apple juice or cider.
Cover and cook on full power for 5
minutes.
3. Meanwhile, sprinkle inside fish
with a little seasoned flour. Roll them
up loosely from tail to head and place
close together in a fairly deep oven
dish.

4. Pour over apple juice or cider. Then sprinkle with pickling spice and add bay leaves. Spread the onion over fish.
5. Cover and cook on full power for 10 minutes.
6. Remove from microwave and allow to cool in the liquid.

Serve cold with hot boiled potatoes or brown bread and butter.

Sybil Norcott
Irlam, Nr Manchester

A tip

Cleaning the microwave cooker. Wipe over regularly with a damp, soapy cloth. For congealed fat, bring a small container of water to the boil on full power. The steam will soften it so that it can be cleaned easily.

Joan Tyers

PORTLAND-STYLE MACKEREL

Serves 4

Nice also with herring.

4 fresh mackerel
Wholewheat flour, seasoned
  with salt and pepper

Gooseberry Sauce

225 g/8 oz gooseberries, fresh or
  frozen
4 tablespoons water, required
  only if gooseberries are fresh
  not frozen
Green colouring (optional)
50 g/2 oz sugar
25 g/1 oz butter
A pinch of nutmeg

1. If you have to bone mackerel yourself this is the way to do it. Gut and clean, removing head and tail. Cut open to backbone from belly to tail. Open out slightly and place on a board, cut side down. Bang hard with a rolling pin along the backbone until mackerel is flat. Turn fish over and backbone just pulls out, bringing most

of the other bones as well. Pull out any long rib bones remaining. Trim off fins and tiny spines. Wash fish and pat dry.
2. Put the gooseberries and water if needed in a medium-sized (1.2 litre/2 pint) bowl. Cover and cook on full power for 4 minutes. Stir halfway through cooking.
3. Put gooseberries through a sieve and then return purée to the bowl.
4. Add sugar, butter and nutmeg and cook for 4 minutes.
5. Stir to dissolve sugar. Add a drop of green colouring if you think it is too pale.
6. Dust mackerel with seasoned wholewheat flour.
7. Grill until golden brown, 4 to 5 minutes each side. Time varies according to size of fish.

Serve sauce separately.

John Firrell
Piddletrenthide, Dorset

SALMON MOUSSE

It is nice to use a fish-shaped mould for this.

Serves 4

A 212 g/7½ oz can of salmon
1 dessertspoon tomato purée
2 tablespoons water
1 tablespoon vinegar
15 g/½ oz gelatine
1 egg-white
A 175 g/6 oz can of evaporated
  milk, refrigerated for 1 hour
  before using
1 teaspoon lemon juice

Decoration

A little paprika pepper
1 stuffed olive
2 gherkins

1. Lightly oil a suitable 850 ml/1½ pint mould.
2. Drain liquid from can of salmon into a cup.
3. Flake salmon, removing bones and dark skin. Mash it with tomato purée.
4. Put the water, vinegar and salmon liquid into a small cup or bowl and sprinkle on the gelatine. Cook on full power uncovered for 10 to 15 seconds.

Do not allow to boil. Stir until completely dissolved.
5. Whisk egg-white until firm.
6. In another bowl whisk cold evaporated milk until thick, adding lemon juice to help it thicken.
7. Stir gelatine into salmon. Fold in whisked milk, and then egg-white. Mix all together gently.
8. Pour into mould and leave 3 to 4 hours to set in a cool place. Goes a bit tough if it sets too quickly.
9. Turn out on to a flat dish. Sprinkle a little paprika pepper down the centre, place half a stuffed olive for the eye, and gherkins, sliced part-way and fanned out, for fins.

Dorothy Sleightholme

SOLE ON A BED OF PASTA SHELLS WITH PRAWNS AND CREAM SAUCE

Serves 4

175 g/6 oz pasta shells
100 g/4 oz butter
Salt and pepper
8 small fillets of sole
50 g/2 oz flour
300 ml/½ pint milk
4 tablespoons dry sherry
150 ml/5 fl oz single cream
1 teaspoon anchovy essence or sauce
50 to 100 g/2 to 4 oz frozen prawns
To garnish: 2 tomatoes, lemon slices

1. Put pasta on to cook in a saucepan of slightly salted boiling water on top of stove. Time it so it is done when fish comes out of microwave.
2. Use 50 g/2 oz of the butter and divide it into 8 little pieces.
3. Shake a little salt and pepper on each fish fillet and roll it up around a piece of butter. Place in a shallow casserole dish.
4. Cover and cook on full power for 6 minutes. Re-arrange halfway through cooking so that fish is evenly done.
5. When fish is done, lift it carefully out of dish on to a plate for a moment and reserve fish juices in a cup.

6. Drain pasta, and put it in fish dish. Set fish on top and keep it warm.
7. Now make the sauce. Put the rest of the butter in a large (1 litre/1¾ pint) jug. Cook uncovered for 1 minute or until melted.
8. Mix in the flour. Gradually stir in the milk and the liquid from fish.
9. Cook uncovered for 4 minutes or until thick. Stir every minute to avoid lumps.
10. Add sherry, cream, anchovy essence and prawns. Return jug to microwave and reheat to boiling point so that the prawns are well heated.
11. Pour sauce over fish and garnish with slices of tomato and lemon.

Anne Wallace
Stewarton, Ayrshire

If you would like to cook the pasta shells by microwave, see Tuna Fish Casserole, *page 28.*

For a prawn filling for pancakes, see Savoury Fillings for Pancakes, *page 55.*

SMOKED FISH AND EGG ON TOAST

A snack for 4 people

350 g/12 oz smoked fish fillet
2 eggs
25 g/1 oz butter or margarine
25 g/1 oz wholemeal or white flour
150 ml/¼ pint milk
Black pepper
2 tablespoons chopped parsley
1 teaspoon lemon juice (optional)
Pieces of freshly-toasted crisp wholemeal bread
Mustard and cress

1. Place the fish in a shallow dish. Cover and cook on full power for 4 minutes. Set aside covered.
2. Boil eggs conventionally in a saucepan of water on top of stove for 10 minutes.
3. Drain liquid from fish into a measuring jug and save 150 ml/¼ pint.
4. Flake fish into fairly large pieces, removing skin.

26

5. When eggs are done, plunge them into cold water and remove the shells. (Held under a running cold tap the eggs will not burn your fingers while you shell them.)
6. Roughly chop eggs and put them with flaked fish.
7. Put the butter or margarine in a large (1 litre/1¾ pint) jug. Cook uncovered for 1 minute or until melted.
8. Blend in the flour. Gradually add the milk and fish liquid. Cook for 4 minutes or until thick. Stir halfway to avoid lumps.
9. Add fish, egg, a grating of black pepper, the parsley and lemon juice. Reheat for 1½ to 2 minutes.

Serve on or with crisply-toasted wholemeal bread and have mustard and cress with it.

Mary Watts

A tip

To toast almonds. For trout and other savoury garnishes. Heat 25 g/ 1 oz butter in a 1 litre/1¾ pint bowl or jug for 30 seconds, uncovered. Stir in 100 g/4 oz flaked almonds. Cook uncovered on full power for 4 to 5 minutes, stirring twice during cooking.

Joan Tyers

FRESH TROUT WITH HERB MAYONNAISE

This is delicious with the trout served hot or cold. A liquidiser is needed for the mayonnaise which is served cold.

Serves 4

4 fresh trout, about 225 g/8 oz each
3 to 4 tablespoons wine vinegar
25 g/1 oz butter

Mayonnaise

1 very small onion or small shallot, very finely chopped
A bundle of fresh herbs; parsley, chervil (or fennel), chives, tarragon, spinach and watercress (or sorrel), about 50 g/2 oz herbs altogether
2 anchovy fillets
1 dessertspoon capers
1 small pickled gherkin
1 hard-boiled egg-yolk
1 fresh egg-yolk
1 teaspoon lemon juice
25 to 50 ml/1 to 2 fl oz sunflower oil
Salt and freshly-ground pepper
To garnish: Lettuce, cucumber slices

1. Leave heads and tails on trout, gut them, wash and wipe out with salt and kitchen paper. Sprinkle inside each trout with wine vinegar and put them in a shallow casserole.
2. Melt butter in a small bowl uncovered on full power for 30 seconds.
3. Brush trout with half of the melted butter. Cover and cook on full power for 9 minutes. Halfway through cooking brush with the remaining butter. If eating trout hot set dish aside covered for 5 minutes. If it is to be served cold allow the trout to get quite cold in the casserole.
4. **For the mayonnaise:** chop the onion or shallot very finely and put it in a cup or small bowl. Cover and cook on full power for 30 seconds. Leave to cool, or to save time empty it into a sieve and hold under running cold water tap.
5. Wash the herbs.
6. Put herbs, onion, anchovy fillets, capers, gherkin, both egg-yolks and lemon juice into a liquidiser.
7. Liquidise for 10 seconds at high speed. Then with liquidiser still in motion start to dribble in the oil, a little at a time, until the mixture thickens and emulsifies.
8. Season with salt and pepper and more lemon juice if necessary.
9. Pour excess juices carefully out of casserole and garnish trout with lettuce and cucumber.
10. Serve mayonnaise separately, giving each person a little pot.

Grace Mulligan

TUNA FISH CASSEROLE

For 2 people, or can be served in ramekins as a starter for 6 people

1.2 litres/2 pints boiling water
1 tablespoon oil
A little salt
125 g/4 oz wholewheat pasta
A 100 g/3½ oz can of tuna fish
1 tin of condensed cream of
  mushroom soup
50 g/2 oz butter
Pepper
A squeeze of lemon juice
  (optional)
1 tablespoon chopped parsley

1. Put the boiling water, oil, salt and pasta in a large (2.75 litre/4½ to 5 pint) bowl. Cover and cook on full power for 12 minutes. Set aside to stand, covered, for 8 minutes.
2. Meanwhile, remove bones from the fish and flake it.
3. Drain the pasta after its standing time and add to it the fish with the soup, butter, pepper and lemon juice. Mix well. Taste for seasoning.
4. Cook covered on full power for 4 minutes. Stir halfway through cooking.
5. Stir in most of the chopped parsley. Turn the mixture into a warmed heat-proof dish and brown it under the grill.

Sprinkle the rest of the parsley on top just before serving.

Anne Wallace
Stewarton, Ayrshire

WHITING WITH MUSHROOMS

Serves 2 or 3

40 g/1½ oz butter

3 or 4 fillets of whiting
50 g/2 oz mushrooms, sliced
1 tablespoon chopped fresh
  parsley
25 to 50 g/1 to 2 oz fresh
  wholewheat or brown
  breadcrumbs*

White sauce

25 g/1 oz butter or margarine
25 g/1 oz flour
300 ml/½ pint milk
Salt and pepper

*White breadcrumbs can be used but then the dish will look nicer if it is browned under the grill at the end.

1. Start with the sauce. Put the 25 g/1 oz butter in a 1 litre/1¾ pint jug. Cook uncovered on full power for 30 seconds.
2. Stir in the flour and gradually blend in the milk. Cook for 4 minutes, stirring frequently to avoid lumps.
3. Use some of the 40 g/1½ oz butter to grease an oven dish.
4. Melt remaining butter in a bowl by cooking uncovered on full power for 30 seconds.
5. Spread white sauce in dish.
6. Lay whiting fillets on sauce. Cover with mushrooms and pour on melted butter.
7. Sprinkle parsley over mushrooms and finish with a layer of breadcrumbs.
8. Cook uncovered on full power for 10 minutes. Let it stand for 2 minutes before serving.

Grace Mulligan

See also Fresh Mussels with Parsley, *page 19 and* Avocado and Salmon Mousse, *page 18*

Chapter 3

Poultry, Game and Rabbit

Some extra useful information, but not necessary for following the recipes.

Most ways of cooking chicken are successful in the microwave cooker, and the recipes chosen for this chapter have been warmly approved by our testers.

Roasting

The important part to remember is the standing time.

If cooked and carved at once the poultry is unpalatable. The standing time enables it to finish by conduction. Depending on personal preference, the poultry and game may or may not be covered and stood on a trivet. Joan Tyers is convinced that meat and poultry taste stewed if not raised out of the juices and left uncovered during cooking (see page 112, P for Poultry).

Times for the full power setting are given below but with variable power settings some people prefer to use a lower (70%) setting and extend the actual cooking time. It is worth checking your manufacturer's instructions, but for general guidance allow on full power:

Poultry	*7 to 8 minutes per 450 g/1 lb*
Duck	*6½ minutes per 450 g/1 lb*
Game birds	*6 minutes per 450 g/1 lb*

See page 112 for Joan Tyers' suggested timings on the lower (roast or 70%) setting.

After cooking wrap the bird tightly in foil and let it stand for 15 to 20 minutes before carving. In order to brown and crisp the skin you may prefer to give that standing time (without wrapping in foil) in a preheated conventional oven (Gas 5, 375°F, 190°C). The bird is cooked when the juices run clear, and this will be evident when standing time is over.

Smaller joints *are best arranged with the thinner areas towards the centre of the container. The standing time for these should be about 5 to 10 minutes. Wrapping in foil is not necessary, but a cover helps to keep the heat in the food.*

Stews and Casseroles

The container should be large enough to avoid boiling over and a cover avoids unnecessary evaporation. The full power setting can be used. However, with game, where the meat is tougher, a lower setting is likely to produce a more tender result. Once the stew or casserole is very hot, reduce the power setting to defrost (30%). If reducing the power the cooking time on this setting would be about 25 minutes per 450 g/1 lb.

Thawing

It is **important to ensure that poultry and game are fully thawed before use.** *Precise timing should be given in your cooker manufacturer's instructions and these should be followed. In the event of the bird not being thawed after the given defrost and standing times it may be left to stand immersed in cold water until no ice remains and the joints are flexible. For guidance, a 1.3 kg/3 lb bird will take between 40 to 60 minutes to achieve total thawing.*

Unless instructions are given to the contrary, the defrost (30%) setting should be used. Whole birds should be turned over once or twice during thawing and smaller joints rearranged.

CHICKEN, BONED, STUFFED AND ROAST

Serves 6

A 1.3 kg/3 lb chicken

1. Using a sharp knife, make a cut through skin and flesh down centre back of bird from neck to tail.
2. Cut and work flesh off body without piercing skin, especially at breast bone where it is thin.
3. For legs, cut off lower limb at joint, then work flesh off thigh and drumstick and pull bones through. Work down shoulders in same way.

Drumstick and wing bones are sometimes left in to help stuffed bird keep a good shape.

Use carcass to make stock (*see page 15*).

The Stuffing

450 g/1 lb pork sausage meat
1 tablespoon finely-chopped parsley
2 chopped shallots (or 1 small onion, finely chopped)
2 tablespoons stock, or wine

Mix all together.

Garnish

4 hard-boiled eggs

Trim a little off the ends so that they will lie close.

To stuff the boned bird

1. Spread the bird out on a board, skin side down.
2. Stuff the legs and shoulders with a little of the stuffing mixture.
3. Spread half the stuffing down the centre of the bird. Place the eggs down the centre end to end. Cover with remaining stuffing.
4. Shape the bird again, stitch with fine string and weigh it.

To cook the stuffed bird

1. Stand the chicken on a trivet or upturned plate in a shallow container. Cook on full power, allowing 8 minutes to the ½ kg/1 lb stuffed weight. Turn over halfway through cooking.
2. Remove the bird, wrap tightly in foil and let it stand for 20 minutes before carving. (Alternatively, remove the bird and cook for 20 minutes in a moderately hot oven, Gas 5, 375°F, 190°C. This will brown and crisp the skin.)

May be eaten hot.

For eating cold:

Coating sauce

50 g/2 oz butter
50 g/2 oz flour
450 ml/¾ pint milk
Salt and pepper
2 tablespoons top of the milk, or cream
150 ml/¼ pint water
25 g/1 oz gelatine

1. Place the butter in a 1 litre/1¾ pint jug. Cook uncovered on full power for 1 minute or until melted. Stir in the flour. Gradually blend in the milk. Cook uncovered for 4½ minutes. Stir every minute to avoid lumps. Set aside.
2. Place the water in a cup. Cook for 1 to 2 minutes until hot.
3. Dissolve gelatine in the water. Reserve one tablespoon of it in a cup and add the rest to the sauce with cream and seasoning.

4. Put through a fine sieve, or even a clean, damp tea cloth, to be sure sauce is smooth. Stir frequently whilst cooking to keep the sauce smooth and velvety. When the consistency of thick cream, it is ready for coating.

Decoration

Any colourful vegetables, peels, etc. (carrot, cucumber skin, lemon/orange peel, gherkin, olives)

1. When the bird is cold, remove strings and skin.
2. Place on a wire tray over a dish. Pour over the coating sauce. Allow to set. Give another coating if necessary (sauce may need rewarming for this).
3. Decorate with small cuttings of colourful vegetables, peels etc., first dipping the pieces in the remaining dissolved gelatine which will stop them slipping off.

CHICKEN SALAD

To cook the chicken

1 chicken, plus giblets
1 small onion, sliced
A piece of carrot, sliced
A piece of celery, chopped
1 small bay leaf
4 peppercorns

For the salad

1 green pepper
3 sticks celery
1 eating apple
Lettuce

The dressing

4 juniper berries
1 large teaspoon curry powder
¼ teaspoon tarragon
¼ teaspoon chervil
2 teaspoons lemon juice
3 large tablespoons
  mayonnaise*

1. Put inside the chicken the giblets, onion, carrot, celery, bay leaf and peppercorns. Stand the chicken on a trivet or upturned plate in a shallow container. Cover.

2. Cook on full power 7 minutes to the ½ kg/1 lb. Remove. Wrap tightly in foil and let it stand for 20 minutes.
3. Unwrap the chicken, remove meat and dice it quite small. Let it cool.
4. To prepare dressing and salad. Crush the juniper berries. Mix them with curry powder, tarragon, chervil and lemon juice. Leave this for 5 minutes.
5. Remove core and seeds from green pepper and cut it up small.
6. Slice celery.
7. Quarter and core the apple, but do not peel it. Cut it up small.
8. Add curry and herbs mixture to the mayonnaise and mix well.
9. Mix together chicken, green pepper, celery, apple and dressing.
10. Lay lettuce leaves on a serving dish and spoon the chicken mixture on to them.

See Cooked Salad Dressing (page 72) for an alternative to mayonnaise.

Mrs M Lucie-Smith
London SW3

BASIC STUFFING FOR POULTRY AND MEAT

This can be made in bulk and frozen without its main seasoning or flavouring ingredients.

700 g/1½ lb onions
50 g/2 oz butter or margarine
350 g/12 oz fresh breadcrumbs,
  wholewheat or white
50 g/2 oz shredded suet
2 lemons, juice and grated rind
1 beaten egg
Salt and pepper

A variety of flavourings, some of which combine well with each other:

Chopped prunes, soaked in
  water overnight
Chopped apricots, soaked
  overnight
Chopped apples
Chopped celery
Chopped herbs like sage,
  parsley, marjoram, thyme, etc.
Chopped nuts

31

1. Peel and finely chop onions. Put them in a large (2.75 litre/4½ to 5 pint) bowl with the butter or margarine. Cover and cook on full power for 13 minutes until soft. Stir halfway through cooking.
2. Allow to cool. Then mix with the rest of the ingredients. Season well.
3. Divide into four: freeze in separate bags.
4. To use, thaw and add the selected flavouring ingredients. The stuffing is then ready to use.

A 275 g/10 oz bag of stuffing may be thawed in the microwave on defrost (or 30%) setting in 4 minutes. Remove from bag and break up with a fork.

Grace Mulligan

PARSLEY AND LEMON STUFFING

Very good with chicken.

50 g/2 oz butter
Finely-grated rind and juice of one lemon
75 g/3 oz fresh brown or white breadcrumbs
4 tablespoons finely-chopped parsley
Pinch of thyme or marjoram
Salt and freshly-milled pepper

1. Place the butter in a 600 ml/1 pint jug. Cook uncovered on full power for 1 minute or until melted.
2. Put all the other ingredients into a basin and mix well.
3. Stir in lemon juice and melted butter until it is well incorporated and the stuffing is moist.
4. Spoon into breast or body of bird. *Or*, spread into a shallow dish and cook uncovered on full power for 2 minutes.

CORN AND BACON STUFFING FOR TURKEY AND CHICKEN

Adjust quantities for size of bird and cavity to be filled. This quantity is enough for 3 to 4 kg/7 to 9 lb turkeys.

Chickens weighing 2.2 to 2.7 kg/5 to 6 lbs need only half the quantity.

50 g/2 oz butter
1 large finely-chopped onion
225 g/8 oz bacon pieces
1 can sweetcorn, approx. 300 g/ 11 oz
4 tablespoons fresh parsley
Salt and pepper
1 teaspoon mixed herbs
1 small loaf of bread, unsliced but crusts removed
2 small beaten eggs

1. Put the butter, onion and bacon in a 2 litre/3½ pint bowl. Cover. Cook on full power for 6 minutes.
2. Add sweetcorn, parsley, salt, pepper and herbs.
3. Cut bread into small cubes and mix in along with beaten eggs.

Do not pack stuffing into bird too tightly. If you prefer it separate rather than inside the bird, this stuffing is best cooked in a conventional oven, moderately hot, Gas 5, 375°F, 190°C, for 30 minutes. It does not cook well by microwave, remaining too moist and not brown or crisp. Cooked in the ordinary oven it remains very pleasant even to eat cold.

Dorothy Sleightholme

A tip

Drying herbs. Wash and dry. Spread on a piece of paper towel on a tray or on microwave turntable. Put in a cup of water alongside herbs. Heat on full power, checking every 30 seconds and picking out the pieces already dry. When dry, rub between fingers and store in airtight jars. The cup of water is there as a precaution in case the herbs on their own pass a 'no load' message to your microwave cooker.

Joan Tyers

CEYLON CHICKEN CURRY

Mostly cooked by microwave, but to obtain the authentic taste of spices a frying pan is also required.

Serves 4 to 5

A 1.3 kg/3 lb chicken, jointed
2 large onions
2 tablespoons ground coriander
2 teaspoons ground cumin
1 teaspoon chilli powder
½ teaspoon turmeric
½ teaspoon cardamom powder
A 5 cm/2 inch piece of cinnamon bark, or ¼ teaspoon ground cinnamon
2 teaspoons salt
4 cloves of garlic, finely-chopped
4 tablespoons vegetable oil
50 g/2 oz creamed coconut
350 ml/12 fl oz hot water
Juice of 1 lemon
2 tablespoons finely-chopped fresh coriander leaves, if you can get them.

1. Place the chicken joints in a large (2.75 litre/4½ to 5 pint) bowl, or the dish from which it will be served. Cover. Cook on full power for 10 minutes. Rearrange halfway through cooking.
2. Meanwhile, grate one of the onions and mix with the spices and salt.
3. Finely-slice second onion and fry with garlic in the heated oil until golden brown.
4. Add grated onion and spice mixture to frying pan and cook gently for about 5 minutes, stirring often.
5. Add chicken joints and fry for another 5 minutes until well-coated with mixture in pan.
6. Dissolve creamed coconut in the hot water and add to chicken.
7. Put all the ingredients back into the large bowl or serving dish. Cover. Cook on full power for 10 minutes.
8. Before serving, add the lemon juice and garnish with the coriander leaves if available.

Serve with boiled rice, rice sticks or noodles.

Priya Wickramasinghe
Cardiff

A tip

If the curry smell lingers in the microwave even after wiping it out in the usual way, it should be reduced by boiling a cup of water to which 1 to 2 tablespoons lemon juice have been added. If not, wiping with a solution of a sterilising agent such as Milton should do the trick.

CHICKEN CASSEROLE

The chicken is browned in a frying pan. Cooking is then completed by microwave.

Freezes well.

Serves 4

50 g/2 oz butter or margarine
4 chicken joints
1 onion, finely-chopped
2 sticks celery, finely-chopped
225 g/8 oz long grain brown or white rice
A 400 g/14 oz tin of tomatoes
600 ml/1 pint hot stock
1 large teaspoon mixed herbs
1 level teaspoon sugar
125 g/4 oz mushrooms, sliced

If brown rice is used lift chicken out of bowl after paragraph 3. At paragraph 4 let tomatoes, stock, rice, etc., cook for 25 minutes. Then replace chicken joints on top of rice for 5 minutes more.

1. Heat butter or margarine in a frying pan and brown the chicken joints. Lift them out of fat on to a plate.
2. Pour the fat into a large (2.75 litre/4½ to 5 pint) bowl and stir in the onion and celery. Cover and cook on full power for 5 minutes.
3. Add rice and mix with onion and celery, making sure rice grains are coated with fat.

33

4. Stir in tomatoes, hot stock, herbs, sugar, salt and pepper. Cover and cook on full power for 12 minutes.

5. Add chicken joints. Cover. Cook for 15 minutes on full power. Turn chicken over halfway through cooking and stir the rice.

6. Stir in mushrooms. Cover and cook for a further 5 minutes.

Dorothy Sleightholme

To make stock in the microwave cooker see page 15.

COUNTRY CHICKEN CASSEROLE

Although this dish is cooked by microwave, the chicken is first browned in an ordinary frying pan on the hob to give it a good colour.

Serves 4

1 medium-sized, sliced onion
50 g/2 oz streaky bacon
4 chicken joints
1 level tablespoon flour,
  seasoned with salt and pepper
125 g/4 oz pork sausage meat
225 g/8 oz tinned tomatoes
½ teaspoon oregano, marjoram
  or mixed herbs
150 ml/¼ pint stock (if necessary)
Chopped parsley

1. Put the bacon and onion in a large (2.75 litre/4½ to 5 pint) bowl. (Or the casserole can be cooked in the dish from which it is to be served, provided it is large enough for the sauce not to boil over.) Cover. Cook on full power for 4 minutes.

2. Dust chicken joints well with seasoned flour.

3. Heat the fat in a frying pan, put in the chicken joints, skin side down, and turn them over in pan until they are golden.

4. Put them into the bowl of bacon and onion. Cook covered for 10 to 12 minutes. Rearrange halfway through cooking. If using drumsticks 10 minutes will be enough, but if joints are larger 12 minutes may be necessary.

5. Meanwhile, divide sausage meat into 8 small balls, roll in the seasoned

flour and fry briskly to seal and brown. Place in between joints in bowl.

6. Measure fat in frying pan. Remove some, or add a little, so that there is just 1 tablespoon. Add remaining flour.

7. Stir to cook flour for 1 minute, then add tin of tomatoes, herbs and as much stock as necessary to make a thick sauce. Stir until boiling.

8. Pour hot sauce over chicken, cover and cook for 8 to 10 minutes. Sprinkle with parsley and serve with plain boiled or new potatoes.

Dorothy Sleightholme

Standing time. As a general rule of thumb, allow one third of the cooking time. All foods require it but the denser the food the longer it takes.

Joan Tyers

CREAMED CHICKEN WITH MUSHROOMS AND BUTTER BEANS

Freezes well.

Serves 4

½ small green pepper
½ small red pepper
1 small onion
2 tablespoons cooking oil
175 to 225 g/6 to 8 oz cooked
  chicken flesh
125 g/4 oz small white
  mushrooms
175 g/6 oz canned butter beans,
  drained
1 glass sherry
2 to 3 tablespoons double cream
Seasoning
To garnish: finely-chopped
  parsley

White Sauce

25 g/1oz butter
25 g/1 oz flour

300 ml/½ pint milk
Seasoning

1. Remove core and seeds from green and red peppers and chop flesh finely. Peel and finely chop the onion.
2. Put the peppers, onion and oil in a 2 litre/3½ pint bowl. Cover. Cook on full power for 6 minutes or until peppers are soft.
3. Cut chicken flesh into bite-sized pieces. Wipe mushrooms with a damp cloth and slice them.
4. Add the chicken, mushrooms, butter beans, sherry, cream and salt and pepper to the bowl. Cover. Cook on full power for 4 minutes. Set aside, covered.
5. **To make the white sauce:** put the butter in a 1 litre/1¾ pint jug. Cook uncovered on full power for 1 minute or until melted.
6. Stir in the flour. Gradually mix in the milk. Cook for 4 minutes. Stir every minute to avoid lumps. Season to taste.
7. Mix white sauce into chicken mixture and turn it out into a serving dish. Cover and reheat on full power for 4 to 5 minutes.
8. Sprinkle with finely-chopped parsley just before serving.

Serve with a green vegetable.

Jean Welshman
Malton, East Yorkshire

Shallow dishes are generally best for microwave cooking. Things will cook faster. Round rather than square, oval rather than rectangular. Food in corners tends to over-cook.

Joan Tyers

CHICKEN WITH TOMATO RICE

This dish is mostly made in the microwave cooker, but the grill is used to brown the chicken and give the dish a good appearance.

Serves 4

2 medium-sized onions
25 g/1 oz butter
225 g/8 oz long-grain rice
A 400 g/14 oz can of tomatoes
600 ml/1 pint hot chicken stock
(a stock cube will do)
2 teaspoons Worcestershire sauce
Salt and pepper
225 g/8 oz packet of frozen mixed vegetables
4 large chicken joints
2 teaspoons oil
To garnish: watercress

1. Peel and slice onions.
2. Put the onions and butter into a large (2.75 litre/4½ to 5 pint) bowl. Cover. Cook on full power for 5 minutes.
3. Stir in rice, tomatoes, hot stock, Worcestershire sauce, salt and pepper. Cook covered for 9 minutes.
4. Stir in frozen vegetables and continue cooking, covered, for a further 8 minutes. Set aside, covered.
5. Brush chicken joints with oil. Brown under pre-heated grill. Place joints on a shallow dish. Cook covered for 10 minutes. Rearrange after 5 minutes to ensure even cooking.
6. Arrange rice and chicken on a warmed dish and garnish with watercress.

Dorothy Sleightholme

CHICKEN WITH TOMATOES AND YOGHURT

A combination of frying pan and microwave is used for this dish.

Serves 4

1 large onion
25 g/1 oz plain flour
1 level teaspoon salt
1 level teaspoon paprika
4 chicken joints
25 g/1 oz margarine
A 400 g/14 oz can of peeled tomatoes

150 ml/¼ pint water
1 level teaspoon sugar
150 g/5 fl oz natural yoghurt
1 tablespoon chopped parsley

1. Peel and thinly slice onion.
2. Mix flour, salt and paprika together.
3. Trim chicken joints and coat in seasoned flour.
4. Melt margarine in a large frying pan. Fry chicken joints until lightly browned, then lift out into a large (2.75 litre/4½ to 5 pint) bowl or use the dish from which it is to be served.
5. Cover bowl and cook on full power for 12 minutes. Rearrange halfway through cooking to make sure joints are evenly cooked.
6. Fry onion for 2 minutes in remaining fat in pan.
7. Stir any remaining flour into pan. Add tomatoes, water and sugar. Bring to boil, stirring.
8. Pour hot sauce over chicken. Cover and cook for 6 minutes.
9. Just before serving, spoon yoghurt over chicken joints and sprinkle with chopped parsley.

Dorothy Sleightholme

CHICKEN IN WHITE WINE WITH TOMATOES

This is the well-known Poulet Chasseur and works very well in the microwave, although a frying pan is used to brown the chicken joints.

Serves 6

1 chicken, jointed, or 6 chicken pieces
2 tablespoons seasoned flour
50 g/2 oz butter or 2 tablespoons oil
450 ml/¾ pint chicken stock
1 large onion, chopped small
A clove of garlic, crushed
Salt and pepper
A 400 g/14 oz tin of tomatoes
1 tablespoon tomato purée
1 teaspoon soya sauce
A dash of Worcestershire sauce
A small glass of dry white wine

1. Roll chicken pieces in seasoned flour and brown in the butter and oil in a frying pan. Remove from pan.
2. Add 1 tablespoon of remaining flour to pan, stir in the chicken stock carefully and allow to thicken on a low heat.
3. Add seasoning, tomatoes, purée, soya sauce, Worcestershire sauce and wine.
4. Meanwhile put onion and garlic into a large (2.75 litre/4½ to 5 pint) bowl. Cover. Cook on full power for 3 minutes.
5. Add the chicken. Cover. Cook for 20 minutes. Rearrange joints twice during cooking.
6. Add the sauce. Cover. Cook for 10 minutes.

Mrs Patricia Chantry
Hook, Goole, N. Humberside

SPICY CHICKEN JOINTS

Uses the microwave cooker and frying pan.

Serves 4

4 large chicken joints
25 g/1 oz butter
1 tablespoon oil
2 large onions, finely-chopped
1 green pepper, de-seeded and chopped
A clove of garlic, finely-chopped
2 teaspoons dry mustard
2 tablespoons tomato purée
300 ml/½ pint hot chicken stock
25 g/1 oz soft brown sugar
3 tablespoons vinegar
1 teaspoon Worcestershire sauce
½ teaspoon salt
1 large sprig fresh tarragon, or ½ teaspoon dried

1. Skin the chicken joints.
2. In a pan, combine butter and oil. Fry chicken joints on all sides until brown.
3. Drain butter and oil remaining in frying pan into a large (2.75 litre/4½ to 5 pint) bowl. Mix in the onion, green pepper and garlic. Cover. Cook on full power for 5 minutes. Add the chicken.
4. Mix mustard into tomato purée and add hot stock, sugar, vinegar,

Worcestershire sauce and salt. Lastly, add the tarragon. Stir until sugar is dissolved. Pour over the chicken.

5. Cover and cook for 15 minutes. Rearrange halfway through cooking to ensure chicken is evenly done.

Grace Mulligan

ROAST DUCKLING WITH WALNUT SAUCE

Serves 4

For the best results in both taste and appearance, the duck is first cooked by microwave, then browned and crisped either under the grill or in the ordinary oven, pre-heated to hot.

A 2 kg/4 to 4½ lb duckling
Salt

Sauce

2 tablespoons duckling dripping
1 medium-sized onion, chopped
50 g/2 oz walnuts, chopped
1 level tablespoon plain flour
300 ml/½ pint duckling stock,
    made by simmering the giblets
    in about 450 ml/¾ pint water
    with a piece of onion
Grated rind and juice of 1
    orange
2 tablespoons sherry
2 tablespoons chopped parsley

To serve and garnish

1 tablespoon duckling dripping
25 g/1 oz walnut halves
Watercress
1 orange, cut into slices

1. Wipe duckling dry inside and out. Prick the skin all over with a fork. This allows the fat to flow out during cooking and bastes the bird without any attention.

2. Place the duck breast-side down on a trivet in a shallow container. Cook covered on full power. Allow 5½ to 6 minutes per ½ kg/1 lb. Halfway through cooking, turn it over and pour off juices.

3. Wrap duck tightly in foil. Let it stand for 15 minutes. If desired, brown under a preheated grill.

Alternatively, when the duck is taken from the microwave cooker, put it straight into a roasting tin and into the ordinary oven, preheated to hot, Gas 7, 425°F, 220°C. It should brown and crisp nicely within the 15 minutes allowed for standing.

4. To prepare sauce. Heat the dripping in a pan, add chopped onion and chopped walnuts and cook gently until lightly browned.

5. Stir in flour and cook for 1 minute.

6. Gradually blend in stock, orange rind and juice and simmer gently for 2 to 3 minutes, stirring throughout.

7. Stir in sherry and chopped parsley and season to taste.

8. To serve. (a) Gently fry walnut halves in duckling dripping then drain well on kitchen paper.

(b) Put duckling on a hot serving dish and garnish with watercress, fried walnuts and orange slices. Serve walnut sauce in a separate bowl.

Audrey Hundy
Abbots Morton, Worcestershire

TURKEY OR CHICKEN PÂTÉ

Serves 4

1 large chopped onion
50 g/2 oz butter
350 g/12 oz cold cooked turkey or
    chicken, in pieces
4 tablespoons cream
1 to 2 tablespoons dry sherry
Salt and pepper
Parsley to garnish
A little extra butter

1. Put the onion and butter in a 1 litre/1¾ pint jug or bowl. Cover. Cook on full power for 5 minutes or until the onion is soft.

2. Mix in turkey or chicken and mince mixture finely (a blender or food processor may be used but mincing gives the smoothest result).

3. Add cream and just enough sherry to moisten. Season to taste with salt and pepper. Beat until smooth.

4. Turn the pâté out into a dish and fork the top. Garnish with parsley.

Or, press into small pots, smooth tops and cover with a thin film of melted butter. To do this, put the extra butter in a 600 ml/1 pint jug. Cook uncovered on full power for 15 to 30 seconds.

Keeps in refrigerator for three days or freezes well for up to three months.

Dorothy Sleightholme

TURKEY AND HAM LOAF

A good way to use up left-over turkey and ham. Easier and quicker by far to cook by microwave than in the conventional oven.

To eat hot or cold.

Serves 6

325 g/12 oz cold cooked turkey
225 g/8 oz ham
1 small chopped onion
1 teaspoon mixed herbs
Salt and pepper
1 large beaten egg
1 teacup fresh breadcrumbs
Stock, if necessary
Browned, dried breadcrumbs for
** coating**

1. Mince turkey, ham and onion, or use a food processor.
2. Add herbs, a very little salt, pepper, beaten egg and fresh breadcrumbs. Use stock if mixture is very dry.
3. Pack into a greased ring mould. Cover.
4. Cook on full power for 7 minutes. Let it stand covered for 5 minutes.
5. Turn out and coat while hot in browned crumbs.

Dorothy Sleightholme

MRS HART'S TURKEY IN A CHEESE AND SHERRY SAUCE

Can also be made with chicken.

Serves 4

325 g/12 oz cold cooked turkey or
** chicken, in bite-sized pieces**
40 g/1½ oz butter
50 g/2 oz wholemeal or white
** flour**

300 ml/½ pint milk
4 tablespoons stock from the
** bird or from a chicken stock**
** cube**
2 tablespoons sherry
Nutmeg
Salt
Black pepper, quite a lot
3 tablespoons grated Parmesan
** and/or Gruyère cheese***
2 tablespoons cream
Fresh or fried breadcrumbs

*To economise Cheddar cheese could be used instead of Parmesan or Gruyère.

1. Remove skin and bone from meat.
2. Put butter in a 1 litre/1¾ pint jug. Cook uncovered on full power for 1 minute or until melted.
3. Stir in the flour.
4. Warm the milk and stock by cooking uncovered on full power for 1 minute. Gradually stir into sauce.
5. Cook for 4 minutes.
6. Add sherry, nutmeg and seasonings. Cook for 1 minute, beat in 2 tablespoonfuls of the cheese and the cream. Set aside.
7. Put the turkey or chicken in a 2 litre/3½ pint bowl. Cover. Cook on full power for 4 minutes or until hot.
8. Put a layer of meat in a shallow oven dish. Pour over a layer of sauce. Fill dish with layers of meat and sauce.
9. Sprinkle with breadcrumbs and remaining cheese.
10. Finally, put under grill to brown before serving.

A tip

Dried breadcrumbs. Cut 4 or 5 slices of bread into fingers, including crusts. Put them into microwave cooker on a piece of paper towel. Heat on full power for 3 minutes. Leave to cool, crumble and store in a screw-top jar.

Joan Tyers

ROAST PHEASANT

Serves 3 to 4

1 pheasant
Half a cooking apple
15 g/½ oz butter
3 or 4 rashers streaky bacon

Accompaniments

Bread sauce, *page 70*
Breadcrumbs, toasted, *page 108*
Brown gravy, *page 71*
Watercress

1. Put inside the pheasant the apple and butter and spread bacon rashers over it, securing with wooden cocktail sticks.
2. Weigh the bird and calculate cooking time at 8 minutes per 450 g/1 lb.
3. Put it on a rack or upturned plate in a shallow dish. Do not cover. Cook on full power. As pheasants vary in toughness you may find by experience that a lower power setting is preferable.
4. Wrap tightly in foil, shiny-side-in, and let it stand for 8 minutes.

Joan Tyers

PHEASANT CASSEROLE

This is a well-flavoured dish and a very satisfactory way to prepare a pheasant of uncertain age. It was described as 'Excellent' when tested for this book.

Serves 2 or 3

50 g/2 oz seedless raisins
150 ml/¼ pint cider (or home-made white wine)
1 pheasant, about 1.1 kg/2½ lb
450 ml/¾ pint of water
A small piece of carrot
1 medium-sized onion
2 sticks of celery
1 medium-sized cooking apple and 1 dessert apple
65 g/2½ oz butter
15 g/½ oz cornflour
Salt and pepper
A pinch of mixed spice
150 ml/¼ pint yoghurt or cream

1. Put raisins to soak in cider or wine for 2 hours.
2. Remove giblets from pheasant and make stock in a saucepan with a lid, on top of stove in the conventional way: simmer them in the water for ¾ hour with the carrot, a quarter of the onion and a small piece of the celery. Then drain off 300 ml/½ pint of stock to use later.
3. Meanwhile, joint the pheasant and sprinkle with salt, pepper and mixed spice.
4. Chop remaining onion and celery finely. Peel, core and chop cooking apple.
5. Put the onion, celery and 25 g/1 oz of the butter into a large (2.75 litre/4½ to 5 pint) bowl. Cover. Cook on full power for 6 minutes.
6. Add the pheasant. Cover and cook for 12 minutes. Turn the joints around halfway through cooking and add the cooking apples.
7. Mix the cornflour with a little cider. Remove the pheasant from the bowl and stir in the cornflour mixture, cider, raisins and stock. Cook uncovered for 4 minutes.
8. Replace the pheasant in the bowl. Cover. Reduce microwave setting to defrost (30%) and cook for 20 minutes. Then stir in yoghurt or cream and turn the casserole out on to a warmed serving dish.
9. Meanwhile, peel dessert apple, cut out core and slice into fine rings. Fry these lightly in a frying pan in the remaining butter and set them on dish around the pheasant.

Serve with bread sauce (*see page 70*), watercress and pieces of lemon.

Mary Watts

CASSEROLED WOOD PIGEON

Serves 4

25 g/1 oz lard
50 g/2 oz belly pork, finely-diced
4 pigeons
225 g/8 oz onions, cut in wedges
1 clove of garlic, crushed
2 sprigs of thyme

25 g/1 oz wholemeal or white
flour
300 ml/½ pint stout (not a sweet
variety – Guinness is best)
300 ml/½ pint hot chicken stock
(or dissolve 1 chicken stock
cube in 300 ml/½ pint boiling
water)
125 g/4 oz mushrooms, sliced
Salt
Black pepper
Gravy browning

1. Melt lard in a frying pan and fry
pork until the fat has run out and a
pale golden colour. Lift pieces out into
a large (2.75 litre/4½ to 5 pint) bowl.
2. Brown pigeons, skin-side down, in
the fat, then add to pork.
3. Add the onions, garlic and thyme to
the bowl. Cover. Cook on full power
for 8 minutes. Turn the pigeons over
halfway through cooking.
4. Remove the pigeons. Stir in the
flour. Gradually add the stout and hot
stock.
5. Add the mushrooms, salt, pepper
and a little gravy browning. Return
the pigeons. Cover and cook for 15
minutes on full power.
6. Reduce to defrost (30%) setting.
Continue cooking for 45 minutes to 1
hour or until tender.

Mary Berry

Suet and 'steamed' puddings.
Always remove plastic wrap or cling-
film as soon as pudding comes out of
microwave cooker. Otherwise it can
contract and squash the pudding into
a tough ball.

Joan Tyers

RABBIT AND BACON PUDDING

This works beautifully by microwave,
saving time and reheating
satisfactorily if necessary. However,

40

do not try to pre-cook the rabbit by
microwave. The flesh remains rubbery
whatever you try. The suet crust looks
lovely if half wholewheat flour is used.
Using only white flour the result does
not look appetizing.

Serves 4

About 675 g/1½ lb rabbit in joints
1 small onion, chopped
1 bay leaf
6 to 8 peppercorns
Water
225 g/8 oz bacon pieces
A little dripping
1 level tablespoon plain flour,
wholewheat or white
600 ml/1 pint stock, from
cooking rabbit
Salt and pepper
A few drops of gravy browning

Suet pastry

150 g/5 oz self-raising flour, half
wholewheat and half white
A pinch of salt
75 g/3 oz shredded suet
100 ml/3 fl oz water

1. First cook the rabbit with the
onion, bayleaf, peppercorns and water
to cover, until tender and easy to
remove from bones. The pressure
cooker is ideal for this, taking only 15
minutes at pressure.
2. Allow rabbit to cool in the liquid,
then lift out joints and remove flesh
from bones.
3. Cut bacon into bite-sized pieces and
fry gently for 8 to 10 minutes. Leaving
fat in pan, lift out bacon and mix it
with rabbit.
4. If necessary, make up fat in pan to 1
tablespoonful. Stir in flour and let it
sizzle for 1 minute.
5. Gradually blend in stock, bring to
the boil and boil 1 minute. Taste for
seasoning. Add gravy browning if
necessary.
6. Now make the suet pastry.
Mix flour, salt, suet and water to a soft
almost sticky dough.
7. Roll out pastry on a floured board
to a round about 30 cm/12 inches
across.

8. Cut away a segment exactly a quarter of the circle. Shape it back into a ball. It will be used for the lid.
9. The large piece of pastry will now fit a greased 1.2 litre/2 pint basin. Put a square of greased greaseproof paper in bottom. Press pastry in lightly. It may be difficult to handle, but microwave-cooked puddings are best if it is kept almost moist. Holes can easily be repaired once it is in the basin.
10. Put the rabbit mixture and 4 or 5 tablespoonfuls of the gravy into the pastry-lined basin.
11. Roll out the lid to fit. Dampen edges and press it gently on top of pudding.
12. Cover basin loosely with plastic wrap, tucking it securely around the rim, but make a generous balloon of it, as the pudding rises well.
13. Cook on full power for 9 minutes. Turn basin around halfway through.
14. Remove plastic wrap at once, let pudding stand for 3 minutes, then turn it out and serve with the extra gravy and a green vegetable.

Reheat a whole pudding covered on full power for 4 minutes.

Dorothy Sleightholme

Chapter 4

Beef, Lamb, Pork, Ham and Bacon

Some extra useful information, but not necessary for following the recipes.

Roasting

It can be disconcerting if you have had a failure roasting an expensive piece of meat. It will almost certainly have been due to overcooking. It is worth persevering.

The important part of cooking meat, particularly whole joints, in the microwave cooker is the standing time. *If cooked and carved immediately the meat will be unpalatable. The standing time enables meat to finish cooking by conduction.*

Depending upon personal preference, you may or may not wish to cover the meat and stand it on a trivet. Joan Tyers feels certain that a joint tastes stewed unless it is raised out of its juices and remains uncovered during cooking (see page 113, R for Roasting).

Times for the full power setting are given below but, as so many microwave cookers have variable power settings, some people prefer to use a lower (70%) setting and extend the actual cooking time. It is worth checking your manufacturer's instructions, but for general guidance allow, on full power:

Beef rare	*5 minutes per 450 g/1 lb*
Beef medium	*6 to 7 minutes per 450 g/1 lb*
Beef well done	*8 to 9 minutes per 450 g/1 lb*
Pork & Bacon	*8 to 9 minutes per 450 g/1 lb*
Lamb	*7 to 8 minutes per 450 g/1 lb*

See pages 108, 111, 112, for Joan Tyers' suggested timings on the lower (roast or 70%) setting.

After cooking, wrap the joint tightly in foil and let it stand for 15 to 20 minutes before carving. The internal temperature of the meat will continue to rise during this time. In some instances, in order to achieve the browned and crisp appearance you may be used to, you may prefer to give the standing time (without wrapping in foil) in a preheated conventional oven, Gas 5, 375°F, 190°C.

Smaller cuts of meat are best arranged with the thinner ends at the centre of the container. The standing time for these would be about 5 to 10 minutes. Wrapping in foil is not necessary, but cover the dish to keep the food warm.

Stews and Casseroles

The container should be large enough to avoid boiling over, and a cover is advisable to avoid evaporation. Like cooking conventionally, slower cooking is required to tenderize tougher cuts of meat, so once the stew or casserole is very hot you should reduce the power setting to defrost (30%). If you do reduce the power, the cooking time on this setting will be about 45 minutes for 450 g/1 lb meat.

Generally, a standing time is not required when the meat has been cooked until tender on the low setting.

Thawing

It is important to ensure that meat is fully thawed before use. Generally, use the defrost (30%) setting and allow **about 10 minutes to the 450 g/1 lb for a large joint,** *and turn it over halfway through. After this, let it* **stand for 20 minutes,** *or until the meat contains no ice crystals.*

Smaller cuts *are best arranged with the thinner ends facing the centre of the container to avoid overheating. Use defrost (30%) setting and allow* **about 5 minutes per 450 g/1 lb. The standing time is about 5 to 10 minutes.** *Wrapping in foil is not necessary, but a cover does help to keep the warmth in the food. These times would also apply to* **mince and diced meat.** *With these, break the meat up halfway through thawing. The meat is thawed when no ice crystals are present.*

STROGANOFF

Made with beef or pork.

Enough for 6 people, but easy to make less

A 1 kg/2 lb single piece of fillet of beef or pork tenderloin
3 medium sized onions
225 g/8 oz button mushrooms
About 25 g/1 oz butter
A little chopped fresh parsley

Sauce

25 g/1 oz butter
25 g/1 oz plain flour
1 level tablespoon tomato purée
½ level teaspoon nutmeg, freshly grated if possible
600 ml/1 pint hot beef stock
150 ml/5 fl oz yoghurt or soured cream
Salt and pepper

1. Prepare meat, cutting it into strips about 5cm/2 inches long and 1cm/½ inch wide.
2. Peel and chop onions finely.
3. Slice the mushrooms.
4. **Now for the sauce.** Put the butter into a large (1 litre/1¾ pint) jug. Cook uncovered on full power for 1 minute or until melted. Stir in the flour. Gradually add the purée, nutmeg and stock.
5. Cook uncovered for 6 minutes. Stir frequently to avoid lumps. Stir in the yoghurt or soured cream. Season with salt and pepper.
6. Into a large (2.75 litre/4½ to 5 pint) bowl, or the dish from which the Stroganoff is to be served, put the onions and butter. Cook covered on full power for 6 minutes, or longer if necessary to be sure they are cooked.
7. Stir in the mushrooms and meat. Cook covered for 5 minutes. If using pork, cook 1 minute longer.
8. Stir in the sauce. Cook covered for 5 minutes. If using pork, cook 1 minute more. Sprinkle with parsley.

Serve with boiled potatoes or rice (*see pages 63 and 66*).

Grace Mulligan

BEEF OLIVES

The beef olives are browned in a frying pan, but the main cooking is done in the microwave cooker. The result is excellent, and about 1 hour is saved on the time it takes to cook conventionally.

Serves 4

575 g/1¼ lb topside beef cut into 8 thin slices, not less than 8 by 10 cm/3 by 4 inches
8 small slices streaky bacon
25 g/1 oz beef dripping
1 level tablespoon flour

43

300 ml/½ pint stock
1 teaspoon Worcestershire sauce
Gravy browning (optional)

Stuffing

1 small grated onion
50 g/2 oz fresh wholewheat or
  white breadcrumbs
25 g/1 oz shredded suet
1 teaspoon chopped parsley
1 teaspoon mixed herbs
A good grating of pepper
1 egg-yolk

1. **Start with the stuffing.** Put the onion in a small bowl. Cover, cook on full power for 3 minutes. Combine with rest of stuffing ingredients and divide into 8 rolls.
2. Beat slices of beef until thin. A rolling pin is ideal for this.
3. Place a piece of bacon and a roll of stuffing on top of each slice of beef. Roll up and tie with a length of fine string. Or fix each roll with a wooden cocktail stick – easier to remove when serving.
4. Melt dripping in large frying pan. When hot, put in beef rolls and turn over in fat to seal.
5. Pack neatly into a shallow casserole, if possible just large enough to contain them.
6. Stir flour into fat in pan and cook 1 minute. Add stock gradually, stirring to prevent lumps forming. Add Worcestershire sauce. Set aside.
7. Cook the beef olives uncovered for 9 to 12 minutes on full power. Turn over or rearrange halfway through cooking.
8. Pour over the sauce. Cook for a further 4 minutes.
9. Remove strings or cocktail sticks and place rolls on hot serving dish. A few drops of gravy browning can be added to the sauce if a little more colour is required. Trickle 1 to 2 tablespoons over beef olives. Strain the rest into a sauceboat.

Serve with a border of piped, creamed potatoes (*see page 63*).

Alternatively, the dish may be served as it is in the casserole.

Dorothy Sleightholme

44

A tip

Standing time. As a general rule of thumb, allow one third of the cooking time. All foods require it but the denser the food the longer it takes.

Joan Tyers

BEEF CASSEROLE

Remember to start the night before.

Serves 4 to 5

675 g/1½ lb stewing beef

Marinade

3 tablespoons oil
1 tablespoon wine or cider
  vinegar, or lemon juice
1 large wineglass of red wine
1 carrot, sliced in very fine rings
1 onion, sliced in rings
1 teaspoon chopped fresh thyme,
  or ½ teaspoon dried
1 bay leaf

To cook

40 g/1½ oz lard
325 g/12 oz carrots, cut in 1 cm/
  ½ inch slices
450 g/1 lb tomatoes, skinned and
  chopped or a 400 g/14 oz can of
  tomatoes
Salt and pepper
150 ml/¼ pint hot beef stock
675 g/1½ lb potatoes, peeled and
  thinly-sliced

1. Put marinade ingredients in a 600 ml/1 pint jug. Cook covered on full power for 3 minutes or until boiling. Reduce to defrost setting (30%) for 10 minutes. Leave to cool.
2. Trim meat and cut it into 2.5 cm/1 inch cubes. Put in a basin.
3. Pour cold marinade over meat and leave overnight in refrigerator or a cool place.

4. Strain marinade off meat and reserve it.

5. Put the lard and carrots in a large (2.75 litre/4½ to 5 pint) bowl. Cover and cook on full power for 9 minutes. Stir in the tomatoes and meat. Continue cooking for 4 minutes.

6. Empty bowl into a deep casserole dish. Pour over the marinade, hot stock, salt and pepper.

7. Cover and cook on full power for 15 minutes. Stir after 7 or 8 minutes. Reduce to defrost setting (30%) and cook for 40 minutes.

8. Top with potato slices. Cook uncovered on full power for 15 minutes. If waxy potatoes are used it may take another 3 to 5 minutes for them to cook. If potatoes are cut thick they will also take longer to cook.

9. Brown under grill if desired.

Grace Mulligan

A tip

Salt toughens and causes dehydration of meat and vegetables cooked by microwave. Always salt afterwards for vegetables, or late in cooking for meat. Less salt is needed for vegetables cooked by microwave, because their natural salts are retained as so little water is used.

Joan Tyers

BEEF AND ORANGE STEW

Entirely cooked by microwave, the flavour is excellent and the appearance good.

Serves 6

675 g/1½ lb stewing steak
225 g/8 oz onions
2 carrots
2 small turnips
1 clove of garlic

25 g/1 oz good dripping
25 g/1 oz flour
2 oranges
600 ml/1 pint hot beef stock (can be made with 1 or 2 beef stock cubes)
150 ml/¼ pint cider
Salt and pepper

1. Trim meat and cut into cubes.

2. Peel and chop onions. Scrub carrots, peel turnips and dice them. Crush garlic.

3. Put the onions, carrots, turnips, garlic and dripping into a 2.75 litre/4½ to 5 pint bowl. Cover. Cook on full power for 8 minutes. Stir halfway through cooking.

4. Stir in the flour and meat. Cook covered for 5 minutes. Stir halfway through cooking.

5. Thinly peel oranges and blanch the rind; that is, put it in a small pan on top of stove with 300 ml/½ pint boiling water and simmer for 2 or 3 minutes, then lift out of the pan, saving the water. Cut rind into thin strips. Squeeze juice from oranges.

6. Add half of the sliced rind and the orange juice to the meat and vegetables.

7. Stir in the hot beef stock and blanching water.

8. Cover. Cook on full power for 15 minutes. Reduce to defrost (30%). Continue cooking for a further 50 minutes. Stir once or twice during cooking.

9. Add cider. Check seasoning, adding salt if necessary and some freshly-ground black pepper. Cook uncovered on full power for 10 minutes.

Serve the stew garnished with the remaining slices of orange rind.

Dorothy Sleightholme

STEAK AND KIDNEY PUDDING

Although the pastry is not as good as when this type of pudding is steamed in the conventional way, many people do find it acceptable, especially considering the great saving in time. However, it is essential to serve the pudding at once as the pastry does harden and become unpalatable as it cools.

Serves 4

Filling

25 g/1 oz beef dripping
125 g/4 oz chopped onion
450 g/1 lb lean pie beef, cut into cubes
125 g/4 oz ox kidney, trimmed and cut slightly smaller than the beef
1 level tablespoon flour seasoned with salt and pepper
300 ml/½ pint hot water
2 teaspoons Worcestershire sauce
125 g/4 oz mushrooms

Suet Crust

225 g/8 oz self-raising wholewheat or white flour, or a mixture of both
½ teaspoon salt
125 g/4 oz shredded suet
7 tablespoons water

1. Put the dripping and onion in a 2.75 litre/4½ to 5 pint bowl. Cover and cook on full power for 3 minutes.
2. Toss beef and kidney in seasoned flour, coating well. Then mix into onion. Cook covered for 4 minutes.
3. Add Worcestershire sauce and hot water. Cover and cook for 15 minutes.
4. Reduce to defrost (30%) setting and cook covered for 45 minutes. Stir halfway through cooking.
5. Pour off all but 3 tablespoons of the gravy and mix the sliced mushrooms with the meat. Allow to cool for about 15 minutes.
6. Make the suet crust, mixing flour, salt, suet and water to a soft but not sticky dough.
7. Lightly grease a 1.2 litre/2 pint heat-proof basin.
8. Roll out pastry on a floured board to a round, about 35 cm/14 inches across.

9. Cut away a segment exactly a quarter of the circle. Shape it back into a ball (it will be used for the lid).
10. The large piece of pastry will now fit the basin. Press it in lightly.
11. Put the cooled meat mixture into the pastry-lined basin.
12. Roll out the lid to fit. Dampen edges and fit it on top.
13. Cover loosely with a piece of cling film and press in around rim of basin. It is not essential to prick cling film if it is used loosely.
14. Cook on full power for 7 to 8 minutes. Turn basin around halfway through cooking.

Serve at once with gravy and green vegetables. If it is not eaten immediately the pastry will go hard.

Dorothy Sleightholme

A tip

Suet and 'steamed' puddings.
Always remove plastic wrap or cling-film as soon as pudding comes out of microwave cooker. Otherwise it can contract and squash the pudding into a tough ball.

Joan Tyers

CANNELLONI

Made in microwave cooker, finished under grill. Freezes well.

Serves 4

12 cannelloni tubes, the ready-to-bake variety are easiest to use

Filling

1 medium onion, finely-chopped
A clove of garlic, crushed
2 tablespoons oil

175 g/6 oz minced beef
1 tablespoon tomato ketchup
1 tablespoon Worcestershire
  sauce
1 teaspoon oregano
Salt and pepper
1 beaten egg
A 250 g/9 oz can of spinach,
  drained
1 tablespoon grated cheese

Tomato Sauce

1 dessertspoon cornflour
2 tablespoons milk
About 600 g/1 lb 6 oz tomatoes,
  skinned and chopped (canned
  tomatoes are suitable)
1 tablespoon tomato ketchup
1 teaspoon sugar
1 level teaspoon oregano
1 level teaspoon sweet basil
Salt and pepper

To cover

40 g/1½ oz grated cheese

1. Put the onion, garlic and oil in a
large (2.75 litre/4½ to 5 pint) bowl. Cook
covered on full power for 4 minutes.
2. Stir in the beef, ketchup,
Worcestershire sauce, oregano, salt
and pepper. Cook covered for 4
minutes.
3. Stir in the egg, then the spinach
and cheese.
4. Stuff the tubes with the mixture.
Place in a large, shallow, heat-proof
casserole dish. Set aside.
5. **Now for the sauce.** In a medium-
sized bowl or a large jug, mix the
cornflour with the milk to make a
smooth paste. Mix in the tomatoes and
remaining sauce ingredients. Cook
covered on full power for 8 minutes,
stirring at intervals until it thickens.
6. Pour the sauce over the cannelloni.
Cook covered 13 minutes on full
power.
7. Sprinkle with the grated cheese.
Brown under a preheated
conventional grill.

Elizabeth Mickery
Pudsey, West Yorkshire

CHILLI CON CARNE

Very quick and easy.

Serves 4

1 onion
1 clove of garlic
Pinch of salt
25 g/1 oz good dripping
1 level tablespoon flour
A 225 g/8 oz can tomatoes
2 level tablespoons tomato purée
½ level teaspoon chilli powder
Pinch of dried marjoram or
  oregano
450 g/1 lb minced beef
A 225 g/8 oz can of baked beans

1. Peel onion and chop it finely. Crush
garlic with a little salt.
2. Put the onion, garlic and dripping
in a large (2.75 litre/4½ to 5 pint) bowl.
Cover. Cook for 5 minutes on full
power.
3. Stir in flour and gradually add the
tomatoes, purée, chilli powder and
marjoram or oregano. Stir in the meat.
4. Cook without covering on full
power for 8 minutes. Stir halfway
through cooking.
5. Add baked beans and cook for a
further 4 minutes.

Serve with green vegetables or a green
salad.

Dorothy Sleightholme

MEAT BALLS IN TOMATO SAUCE

This dish freezes well.

Serves 4

450 g/1 lb finely-minced beef
50 g/2 oz fresh wholemeal or
  white breadcrumbs
1 large grated onion
1 beaten egg
1 tablespoon plain flour
1 level teaspoon salt
½ teaspoon pepper
A 400 g/14 oz can of tomatoes,
  chopped roughly
1 tablespoon tomato purée
(optional)

47

300 ml/½ pint hot beef or bacon stock

1. Mix together beef, breadcrumbs, half the onion and the beaten egg.
2. Form into 16 even-sized balls. Roll them in flour mixed with salt and pepper.
3. Place meat balls on a plate, arranging them in a ring around edge of plate. (If necessary cook them in two lots.)
4. Cook each plateful uncovered for 4 minutes on full power. Turn them over halfway through cooking. Set aside. If cooking altogether give them 7½ minutes, but rearrange halfway through so that those in the centre of the dish are placed around the edge.
5. Mix the remaining flour with a little juice from the can of tomatoes to make a smooth paste. If necessary, add a little more flour. Stir in the tomato purée and then the tomatoes and remaining juice.
6. Put remaining onion in a small bowl and cook covered on full power for 1½ minutes, or until soft.
7. Arrange the meat balls in a dish deep enough for sauce not to boil over.
8. Pour tomato mixture and hot stock over meat balls. Add the onion. Cover and cook for 10 minutes. Stir halfway through cooking and again after 8 minutes, rearranging meat balls carefully to ensure even cooking.

Serve in a ring of potatoes or rice, with green vegetables. Pour a little sauce over the meat balls, serve the rest separately.

Dorothy Sleightholme

This dish can be taken from the freezer, thawed and reheated by microwave. Allow 30 minutes. Try to use a container which keeps a good depth of sauce around the meat balls. If the container is too large, the sauce will spread out and could result in too much evaporation.

1. **To defrost**, cook covered on defrost (30%) setting for 10 minutes. Increase to full power for 10 minutes. Then let it stand for 10 minutes. Stir and rearrange at 3 or 4 minute intervals to ensure even defrosting.
2. **Reheat** on full power for 5 more minutes, or until all the meat balls are hot.

Remove the meat balls and whisk the sauce a little if it shows signs of curdling.

Marie Emmerson

Round or oval dishes are preferable to square or rectangular ones. The microwaves tend to congregate in corners and this leads to overcooking.

Bunty Johnson
Knutsford, Cheshire

MINCED MEAT CURRY

Very quick and easy. If you want another short-cut, all the ground spices could be replaced by 1 teaspoon curry paste, although the flavour would not be so good.

Serves 4

2 tablespoons oil
1 medium onion, chopped
3 cloves garlic, chopped
2 green chillis, finely chopped
½ teaspoon chopped fresh ginger
A pinch of salt
2 teaspoons ground coriander
2 teaspoons ground cumin
1 teaspoon garam masala*
¼ teaspoon turmeric
450 g/1 lb lean mince
1 teaspoon tomato purée
50 g/2 oz creamed coconut
125 ml/4 fl oz hot water
1 cup fresh or frozen peas

Can be bought at wholefood shops and oriental food shops

1. Put the oil and onions in a large (2.75 litre/4½ to 5 pint) bowl. Cook covered on full power for 3 minutes.
2. Add garlic, chillis, fresh ginger, a pinch of salt and the ground spices.
3. Mix in the meat, breaking up the lumps.
4. Cook covered for 8 minutes. Stir halfway through cooking.
5. Mix in tomato purée.
6. Dissolve creamed coconut in the hot water, mix it in. Cover bowl and cook for 4 minutes.
7. Toss in peas, cover and cook for a further 4 minutes.

Serve with Boiled Rice (*see page 66*). Nice also with Curried Bhindi (*page 57*).

Priya Wickramasinghe
Cardiff

A tip

Smells. If you cannot remove a smell by wiping the cooker with a hot damp cloth and a spot of detergent: put a piece of lemon rind or a dash of lemon juice (bottled variety is suitable) into a small bowl with 300 ml/½ pint water and let it boil uncovered in the microwave cooker on full power for 1 to 2 minutes. Then wipe with a clean tea towel.

Joan Tyers

A RICH MEAT SAUCE FOR SPAGHETTI

This sauce freezes well.

2 rashers streaky bacon
1 onion
A clove of garlic
1 carrot
2 tablespoons oil
1 small pig's kidney
225 g/8 oz beef mince
1 tablespoon tomato purée
150 to 300 ml/¼ to ½ pint stock

A pinch of mixed herbs
Black pepper
Salt
2 teaspoons wholewheat or white flour or cornflour
1 tablespoon water

To serve

Wholewheat spaghetti, if you can get it. A little grated cheese, preferably Parmesan.

1. Remove rinds from bacon and cut it very small.
2. Peel and finely chop onion. Crush garlic. Finely grate the carrot.
3. Put into a large (2.75 litre/4½ to 5 pint) bowl the bacon, onion, garlic, carrot and oil. Cook covered on full power for 6 minutes.
4. Dice the kidney very finely and stir it and the mince into bowl.
5. Cover and continue cooking on full power for 6 minutes. Stir halfway through cooking.
6. Stir in the tomato purée, 150 ml/¼ pint stock, herbs, pepper and salt. Cook covered for 4 minutes.
7. Meanwhile, cook spaghetti in the usual way on top of the stove in plenty of boiling salted water*.
8. Thicken meat sauce at last minute, if necessary, by mixing flour and water, stirring in and bringing back to the boil on full power. Stir to avoid lumps.

Serve the grated cheese separately in a small bowl.

Dorothy Sleightholme

*See page 66 to cook spaghetti by microwave and to reheat it from frozen state.

ROAST LAMB WITH APRICOT STUFFING

Remember to start this dish the night before serving.

Serves 4 to 6

50 to 75 g/2 to 3 oz dried apricots
50 g/2 oz butter or margarine
1 medium-sized onion
50 g/2 oz fresh wholemeal or white breadcrumbs

1 tablespoon chopped parsley
Salt and pepper
150 ml/¼ pint stock
1 egg-yolk
900 g/2 lb boned shoulder of lamb
A little dripping

1. Put apricots to soak in water overnight.
2. Next day, drain and cut them up quite small.
3. Put the butter and onion in a medium-sized (2 litre/3½ pint) bowl. Cover. Cook on full power for 4 minutes.
4. Mix in the apricots, breadcrumbs, parsley, salt and pepper. Moisten with 1 to 2 tablespoons stock.
5. Beat egg-yolk and add it to stuffing with a little more stock, if necessary, to make it moist but not sticky.
6. Fill the pocket in the lamb with the stuffing and tie it up with string.
7. Put joint in a shallow dish and cook uncovered on full power for 9 minutes per 450 g/1 lb. Turn it over halfway through cooking.
8. Wrap tightly in foil and leave it to stand for 10 minutes.
9. Brown under a preheated grill, if necessary.

Mrs Emily Williams
Moggerhanger, Bedfordshire

To rehydrate *dried apricots* without soaking overnight. Put 225 g/8 oz dried apricots in a dish, cover with water. Cover dish and cook on full power for 4 minutes then leave to stand for 3 minutes.

Joan Tyers

HONEYED WELSH LAMB

Oen Cymreig melog

Good Welsh lamb needs no dressing up and is amongst the best and least

adulterated meat that can be bought in Britain. This recipe gives a spicy gloss to the joint and a delicious gravy.

Serves 6 to 8

A 1.3 to 1.8 kg/3 to 4 lb joint of lamb, preferably the fillet end of the leg
Pepper
1 teaspoon ground ginger
1 dessertspoon dried or 2 sprigs fresh rosemary
2 tablespoons runny honey
About 300 ml/½ pint cider

1. Rub pepper and ginger all over joint and put it on a rack or upturned plate in a shallow dish.
2. Sprinkle rosemary over it and dribble on the honey. Pour cider around it.
3. Cook on full power allowing 8 minutes to each 450 g/1 lb. Baste the meat several times during cooking. Turn it over once.
4. Remove joint, wrap tightly in foil, shiny side in, and let it stand for 15 minutes before carving. The meat will continue to cook by conduction during this time. This standing time is essential, otherwise it will not be pleasant to eat. Instead of wrapping in foil, it can be placed in a pre-heated oven, Gas 5, 375°F, 190°C, for 15 to 20 minutes, which will brown it a little more.
5. Make gravy using residue in roasting dish (*see page 71*).

Mrs Joyce Powell
Llanddewi Rhydderch W.I., Gwent

To make crystallised or very firm *honey* runny again. Put jar (without metal lid) into microwave cooker at full power for 1 to 2 minutes.

Joan Tyers

50

MOUSSAKA

Cooked by microwave and finished under the grill.

Enough for 6

450 g/1 lb aubergines
1 tablespoon salt
Good cooking oil
2 large onions, thinly-sliced
A clove of garlic, crushed
450 g/1 lb lean lamb, from the
  shoulder or leg, minced
A 400 g/14 oz can of tomatoes
2 tablespoons tomato purée
Salt and pepper

Topping

2 eggs
A 142 ml/5 fl oz carton of single
  cream
50 g/2 oz grated Cheddar cheese
25 g/1 oz grated Parmesan
  cheese

1. It is necessary to salt aubergines. (This will help them absorb less oil during cooking.) Wipe, top and tail, cut into 7 mm/¼ inch thick slices and lay out in a colander, sprinkling with 1 tablespoon salt. Leave for one hour. Press gently and pat dry on kitchen paper.
2. Put the aubergines and 1 tablespoon oil in a medium-sized (2 litre/3½ pint) bowl. Stir to coat the slices with oil. Cover and cook on full power for 4 minutes. Set aside.
3. Put 1 tablespoon oil, the onions and garlic in a medium-sized (2 litre/3½ pint) bowl. Cover and cook for 5 minutes. Stir halfway through cooking.
4. Stir in lamb. Cook covered for 4 minutes.
5. Stir in tomatoes, mince, salt and pepper.
6. Arrange alternate layers of aubergine and lamb mixture in a 1.2 litre/2 pint soufflé dish or shallow casserole. Cook uncovered for 5 minutes.
7. Meanwhile, prepare topping. Beat eggs and cream together. Stir in grated cheese.

8. Pour this on top of the moussaka and brown under a preheated grill.

Grace Mulligan

KIDNEYS IN A SAUCE WITH MUSHROOMS

Serves 2

3 lamb kidneys
25 g/1 oz plain flour
Salt and pepper
1 medium-sized onion, chopped
25 g/1 oz lard
50 g/2 oz mushrooms, thickly
  sliced
300 ml/½ pint hot beef stock, a
  stock cube will do
Gravy browning (optional)

1. Remove skins from kidneys, cut them in half and cut out the core. Then chop up, but not too small.
2. Season the flour with salt and pepper. Toss chopped kidneys in it.
3. Put the onion in a small (1.2 litre/2 pint) bowl with the lard. Cover and cook on full power for 4 minutes, or until tender.
4. Stir in the kidneys and mushrooms. Cook covered for 3½ minutes. Stir halfway through cooking.
5. Stir in the remaining flour. Gradually add the stock, and a few drops of gravy browning if you prefer more colour. Cover and cook for 5 minutes. Stir halfway through cooking.
6. Let it stand covered for 3 minutes. Taste and season, if necessary, with more salt and pepper.

Dorothy Sleightholme

LIVER RAGOÛT

Serves 4

450 g/1 lb lamb's or calf's liver
15 g/½ oz seasoned flour
25 g/1 oz dripping

1 finely-chopped onion
Juice of $\frac{1}{2}$ a lemon
5 tablespoons dry red or white
wine
125 g/4 oz mushrooms
Gravy browning (optional)

To serve

675 g/1$\frac{1}{2}$ lb creamed potatoes or
225 g/8 oz Patna rice
Chopped parsley

1. Wash liver, remove skin and any tubes. Cut into 2.5 cm/1 inch pieces.
2. Coat in flour seasoned with a shake of salt and pepper.
3. Put the dripping and onion in a medium-sized (2 litre/3$\frac{1}{2}$ pint) bowl. Cover. Cook on full power for 4 minutes.
4. Stir in the liver. Cook covered on full power for 4 minutes.
5. Add lemon juice, wine and washed and sliced mushrooms. Carefully add a few drops of gravy browning if you think it is too pale. Cook covered on full power for about 6 minutes more until liver is tender.
6. Meanwhile, cook potatoes in a pan on top of stove in the conventional way and beat until creamy. Form into a ring on warm dish, pour ragoût in centre. Sprinkle with chopped parsley.

If using rice, this may be cooked in the microwave. It requires 10 minutes' standing time, during which the ragoût can be cooked.

Potatoes can also be cooked for creaming by microwave (*see page 63, Mashed potatoes*).

Dorothy Sleightholme

CASSEROLE OF PORK

The best results are gained by using an ordinary frying pan and the microwave cooker.

Serves 4

450 to 675 g/1 to 1$\frac{1}{2}$ lb lean pork
slices from the shoulder, about
1 cm/$\frac{1}{2}$ inch thick

1 heaped tablespoon flour,
seasoned with salt and pepper
Dripping for frying
450 g/1 lb onions, sliced
3 or 4 cooking apples
300 to 450 ml/$\frac{1}{2}$ to $\frac{3}{4}$ pint stock or
water
2 tablespoons brown sugar

1. Dip the pork slices in seasoned flour and fry them in a little dripping in the conventional way, in a frying pan on top of the stove. When lightly brown, lift them out into a large casserole.
2. Now fry the onions lightly and put them on top of pork.
3. Core the unpeeled apples and slice into thick rings. Place these on top of onion.
4. Heat the stock or water, covered, on full power for 3 to 4 minutes. Pour it over contents of casserole. Sprinkle with sugar.
5. Cook covered on full power for 10 minutes then reduce to defrost (30%) setting. Cook for 10 minutes, or until meat is tender.
6. Let the casserole stand for 10 to 15 minutes before serving.

Miss G. S. Davies
Flintshire

A tip

Pastry looks better if you use half wholewheat and half white flour. Cooking the pastry with the filling isn't successful. It is possible to cook a pastry case blind, then to cook filling inside ready-baked case. An 18 cm/ 7 inch flan case is the best size for baking blind. Roll out pastry and fit it into flan dish. Prick base and sides, then let it 'relax' in refrigerator for 15 minutes. Cook uncovered on full power for 4 minutes.

Joan Tyers

Reheating mashed potato on a plate of food is not always successful, as microwaves are attracted to the other foods more readily than the potato. It will heat better if it is spread around the plate rather than piled in a mound.

Joan Tyers

PORK IN CIDER WITH WALNUT-STUFFED PRUNES

This dish freezes well for about 3 months. Remember to start the night before.

Serves 4 to 6, but easy to make less

16 prunes
450 to 675 g/1 to 1½ lb diced pork, from the shoulder
1 heaped tablespoon cornflour
1 onion, chopped
1 tablespoon oil
300 ml/½ pint dry cider
300 ml/½ pint hot chicken stock
A clove of garlic, crushed
4 cloves or ¼ teaspoon ground cloves
¼ teaspoon marjoram
Salt and pepper
16 walnut halves

1. Start by pouring boiling water over prunes and leaving to soak and plump up for at least 12 hours. If using ready-softened prunes, soak in cold water.
2. Toss pork in cornflour.
3. Put the onion and oil in a large (2.75 litre/4½ to 5 pint) bowl. Cook covered for 3 minutes.
4. Add meat, cook for 6 minutes. Stir halfway through cooking.
5. Add cider, hot stock, garlic, cloves, marjoram, salt and pepper.
6. Cover. Bring to the boil and cook for 10 minutes. Then reduce to defrost (30%) and cook for 45 minutes or until meat is tender. Depending on the meat

and the size of pieces, you may find it is ready to eat after 30 minutes.
7. Stuff the prunes with walnuts and add to the dish after 25 minutes of slow cooking time.

Mrs Angela Mottram
Axbridge, Somerset

To plump prunes without soaking overnight. Put 225 g/8 oz prunes in a dish, cover with water, cover dish. Cook on full power for 5 minutes. Leave to stand for 5 minutes.

Joan Tyers

SWEET AND SOUR PORK

Pork can sometimes look insipid cooked in the microwave. This dish looks best if the meat is browned in a frying pan.

Serves 4

450 g/1 lb boneless pork, from the shoulder
2 tablespoons cooking oil
1 small green pepper
4 dessert apples
15 g/½ oz butter
1 tablespoon brown sugar
2 teaspoons soya sauce
2 tablespoons orange or pineapple juice
A dash of wine or cider vinegar or Worcestershire sauce
Salt and pepper

1. Cut pork into 1 cm/½ inch cubes and fry in oil over quite a high heat to brown it nicely.
2. Put pork in a medium-sized (2 litre/3½ pint) bowl. Cover and cook for 8 minutes. Stir halfway through cooking. Set aside.
3. Meanwhile, remove core and seeds from green pepper and cut up small.
4. Just before they are required, peel and core apples and cut into 1.5 cm/¾ inch chunks.

5. Put the apples, butter and sugar in a medium-sized bowl with the green pepper. Cook covered for 5 minutes, or until apples are soft.
6. Sprinkle with soya sauce, fruit juice and vinegar or Worcestershire sauce. Stir and check seasoning, adding salt and pepper if necessary.
7. Stir in the pork. Cook covered for 3 minutes.

Serve with plain boiled brown rice (*see page 66*.)

Dorothy Sleightholme

TO COOK A HAM JOINT

1. Soak joint in water for at least 2 hours to remove excess salt.
2. Place on a rack or upturned saucer in a shallow dish. Protect thin end with a small piece of foil to prevent it overcooking.
3. Cook uncovered on full power allowing:
Up to 1.3 kg/3 lb – 10 minutes per 450 g/1 lb
Over 1.3 kg/3 lb to 4 kg/9 lb – 9 minutes per 450 g/1 lb
Remove protective foil halfway through and turn the meat over.
4. After cooking, wrap whole joint in foil, shiny side inwards, and let it stand to complete cooking by conduction for 15 minutes.

Can be glazed before cooking and again halfway through: rub with dark brown sugar and mustard, or runny honey mixed with a little mustard.

Joan Tyers
South Milford, Yorkshire

SAVOURY FILLINGS FOR PANCAKES

Pancakes cannot be made in a microwave cooker. They have to be made first in the conventional way and kept warm or reheated (*see page 111*).

125 g/4 oz plain wholewheat or white flour

½ teaspoon salt
1 large egg
300 ml/½ pint milk
A little butter or oil for cooking

1. Put flour and salt in a bowl and make a well in the centre.
2. Drop in egg and begin to mix, gradually adding 150 ml/¼ pint of the milk as the flour is drawn in from the sides.
3. Gradually beat in remaining milk and beat mixture until bubbles are visible.
4. Put mixture into a jug for easier pouring into the frying pan.
5. Heat frying pan and grease it lightly. Carefully pour in some mixture and tilt pan to let it spread and form a thin pancake. Cook until golden brown underneath and drying on top.
6. Toss or flip over and cook until golden brown.

Savoury fillings

Enough for 8 or 9 small pancakes. To serve 2 or 3 people as a snack or a starter for 4.

Ham

300 ml/½ pint thick basic white sauce (*see page 69*), made, if possible, with ham stock – otherwise a chicken or ham stock cube will do
175 g/6 oz chopped cooked ham
1 dessertspoon cooked peas
½ teaspoon chopped fresh parsley

Mushroom

300 ml/½ pint thick basic white sauce (*see page 69*) using chicken stock
175 g/6 oz chopped, lightly-cooked mushrooms
1 dessertspoon cooked peas

To cook the mushrooms in microwave cooker, put 25 g/1 oz butter in a bowl and cook uncovered on full power for 1 minute, just to melt. Toss the mushrooms in the butter, cover and cook on full power for 3 to 4 minutes. Stir halfway through.

Prawn

300 ml/½ pint thick basic white sauce (*see page 69*), **using stock made from simmering prawn shells in a little water, then making up to 300 ml/½ pint with milk,** *or* **use all milk**
125 g/4 oz prawns
1 hard-boiled egg, chopped
1 dessertspoon chopped fresh parsley

1. First make the sauce.
2. Mix in the other ingredients.
3. Spread filling across the middle of each pancake and wrap it up.
4. Place 3 or 4 filled pancakes on each serving plate and cook each plateful separately, uncovered, on full power for 2 minutes.

Grace Mulligan

TRADITIONAL SUSSEX BACON PUDDING

Serves 2

125 g/4 oz self-raising wholewheat flour
1 teaspoon baking powder
50 g/2 oz shredded suet
1 teaspoon mixed fresh herbs or ½ teaspoon dried
Pepper and a little salt
1 onion, finely-chopped
3 to 4 rashers streaky bacon, chopped
1 medium to small egg
150 ml/¼ pint milk

1. Mix together flour, baking powder, suet, herbs and seasoning.
2. Put the onion in a medium-sized (2 litre/3½ pint) bowl. Cook covered on full power for 3 minutes.
3. Stir in the bacon, cover and cook for a further 2 minutes.
4. Meanwhile, beat egg lightly and add to milk.
5. Quickly stir the onion and bacon into the dry pastry mix and pour on the egg and milk. Mix quickly to a dough of soft, dropping consistency.

6. Grease a 1 litre/1¾ pint pudding basin and put in a piece of greaseproof paper just to cover bottom.
7. Put pudding mixture into basin. Cover loosely with cling film, tucked in neatly under the rim. It is not necessary to prick the top when covering loosely.
8. Cook on full power for 10 minutes.
9. Remove cover and leave pudding to stand for 3 minutes before serving.

Serve with Parsley Sauce (*see page 70*).

Mrs Sheila Powell
Portslade, Sussex

TO KEEP AND USE LEFT-OVER FAT

The fat can be removed from stock after boiling beef, bacon or ham, or from the dripping tin after roasting. But do not mix the fats from different meats.

To clarify

1. Put fat in a bowl with a little water. Bring to the boil uncovered on full power.
2. Strain into a basin and allow to set. All sediment will sink into the water below.
3. The fat can be removed from the top. Scrape clean, melt and pour into labelled pots.

It is advisable to use beef dripping when cooking beef dishes, pork or bacon dripping for pork, etc. In this way the flavour of the meat is not impaired.

Pork and bacon dripping makes good pastry for using with a savoury filling.

Beef dripping is delicious on toast.

Mutton fat will seal chutneys in the same way as wax.

When fat is clarified it will keep, if covered, for several weeks. If not covered, it is inclined to develop an 'off flavour'. Should not be frozen, but will keep in refrigerator.

Chapter 5
Vegetables, Rice and Pasta

Some extra useful information, but not necessary for following the recipes.

Vegetables cook beautifully *in the microwave cooker, but if you prefer very soft vegetables then the conventional method is still the best for you.*

A large container *should be used to ensure the vegetables have plenty of room to spread out and you should use* **a cover** *to reduce the evaporation. Generally, you should use the full power setting. As a rule of thumb, add* **2 to 3 tablespoons water,** *whatever the quantity of vegetables. If the time taken to cook is as little as 6 to 7 minutes, only 2 minutes standing time is necessary, so the time taken to serve will be enough.* **Stir or rearrange** *halfway through cooking for an evenly-cooked result. Incidentally, sprinkling* **salt on uncooked vegetables** *can cause them to* **toughen** *so add such seasonings after cooking.*

Frozen vegetables *are usually thawed and cooked within the same operation, and extra water is generally not required.*

Whole vegetables such as jacket potatoes are best arranged in a circle. Prick their skins to avoid them bursting during cooking.

Rice and pasta *cook well by microwave, but little time is saved as so much water is required. Nevertheless, there is no scorching or steam from boiling water, so less condensation in the kitchen. Use a large, covered container because of the tendency to froth up.*

Rice Puddings *can be cooked in the microwave, but the texture is not the same and a crisp brown skin does not form.*

AUBERGINES AND TOMATOES

This dish looks very attractive. It must, however, be eaten almost at once or the aubergine will discolour.

Serves 4

6 very firm, ripe tomatoes
2 aubergines, fairly large
1 onion, finely-sliced and
  chopped small
A clove of garlic, finely-chopped

$\frac{1}{2}$ level teaspoon fresh basil, or
  a good pinch of dried
1 tablespoon oil
Pepper

1. Put tomatoes in a bowl, cover with boiling water and leave for 30 seconds. Plunge them into cold water and skin after 1 minute.
2. Slice the tomatoes and arrange half of them in a well-greased, shallow oven dish.
3. Wash the aubergines. Trim off stem ends. Cut in half lengthways.

56

4. Now, with skin side up, make lengthways cuts 1 cm/½ inch apart to within 1 cm/½ inch of stem end.
5. Transfer to dish. Space the aubergine fans out in a single layer. Fill the spaces between the fans with slices of tomato.
6. Arrange the rest of the tomatoes, onion, garlic and basil around the fans. Brush all over with oil. Season with pepper.
7. Cover and cook on full power for 13 minutes or until aubergines are tender. Turn dish around halfway through cooking.

Serve on its own as a snack or as an accompaniment to grilled lamb.

Grace Mulligan

To prepare 2 *aubergines* (total weight 350 g/12 oz) for stuffing, and to prevent flesh from going dark. Wash and dry. Prick skin in several places with a fork and put them on a plate. Cook uncovered on full power for 6 minutes. Let them stand for 2 or 3 minutes. They are now ready to scoop out and fill with ready-cooked, hot filling.

Joan Tyers

CURRIED BHINDI

This unusual green vegetable is also known as okra and ladies' fingers. Its shape resembles that of a chilli, and it is best bought when small, with no discolouration. Bhindi is now quite widely available from supermarkets and greengrocers.

Serves 4

450 g/1lb bhindi
1 tablespoon oil
1 small onion, finely-chopped
½ teaspoon ground cumin
½ teaspoon coriander
½ teaspoon chilli powder (optional)
¼ teaspoon ground turmeric
150 g/5 oz canned tomatoes, chopped
½ teaspoon salt

1. Wash and dry the bhindi. Trim the tops and tails and cut into 2.5 cm/ 1 inch pieces.
2. Put the oil, onion and spices in a large bowl. Cook covered on full power for 4 minutes or until onions are tender.
3. Add bhindi and stir until well mixed and coated with spices. Cook covered on full power for 5 minutes. Stir halfway through cooking.
4. Add tomatoes. Cook covered for 4 minutes. Salt if necessary.

Serve with boiled rice (*see page 66*), Chicken Curry (*see page 33*) and onion salad; or with grilled steak, or lamb chops.

If you prefer a **richer curry flavour,** fry the onion and spices in the oil in the conventional way on top of the stove. Then mix with the bhindi in a large bowl or serving dish, and continue as above from paragraph 3.

Priya Wickramasinghe
Cardiff

Smells. If you cannot remove a smell by wiping the cooker with a hot damp cloth and a spot of detergent: put a piece of lemon rind or a dash of lemon juice (bottled variety is suitable) into a small bowl with 300 ml/½ pint water and let it boil uncovered in the microwave cooker on full power for 1 to 2 minutes. Then wipe with a clean tea towel.

Joan Tyers

BROAD BEANS WITH BACON

Can be made in large or small quantities.

450 g/1 lb broad beans –
  prepared weight
2 rashers of bacon, or bacon
  pieces
1 small onion
3 tablespoons water
2 teaspoons cider or tarragon
  vinegar
½ teaspoon sugar
Freshly-ground black pepper
Salt

1. Prepare beans. If they are very young and tender do not pod them. String the pods and cut into 5 cm/ 2 inch lengths.
2. Take rinds off rashers and cut bacon into small pieces.
3. Peel and finely chop onion.
4. Put the beans and water in a large bowl. Cook covered on full power for 6 to 8 minutes, depending on age. Stir halfway through cooking. Set aside, covered.
5. Put bacon and onion in a medium-sized bowl or serving dish. Cook covered for 3 minutes on full power or until soft.
6. Add vinegar, sugar and freshly ground pepper. Cook for 2 minutes.
7. Drain beans, toss them into the bowl with the bacon mixture, add a pinch of salt, mix well and serve at once.

Betty Yeatman
Adelaide, South Australia

BROCCOLI WITH BUTTER SAUCE

Make sure the broccoli is very fresh. The microwave cooker is perfect for sauces.

Serves 3 to 4

3 tablespoons water
450 g/1 lb broccoli sprigs

Sauce

60 g/2½ oz butter
25 g/1 oz flour
300 ml/½ pint boiling water
1 egg-yolk
Salt and pepper
2 teaspoons lemon juice

1. Put the water into a large (2.75 litre/4½ to 5 pint) bowl. Arrange the broccoli with the stalks standing upwards. Cover and cook on full power for 7 minutes. Set aside, covered.
2. Put one third of the butter into a 600 ml/1 pint jug. Cook uncovered for 1 minute. Blend in the flour. Whisk in the boiling water. Cook for 30 seconds. Whisk again. Repeat until the sauce is thick.
3. Beat in egg-yolk and remaining butter.
4. Season to taste and add lemon juice.
5. Pour over cooked broccoli, nicely arranged in a warm dish, or serve in a separate sauce-boat.

If sauce is not served at once it can be reheated, but it is risky doing this in the microwave as it might overheat and curdle. Better to reheat carefully in a bowl over a saucepan of water, or a double saucepan, on top of the stove.

Anne Wallace
Stewarton, Ayrshire

A tip

Salt toughens and causes dehydration of meat and vegetables cooked by microwave. Always salt afterwards for vegetables, or late in cooking for meat. Less salt is needed for vegetables cooked by microwave, because their natural salts are retained as so little water is used.

Joan Tyers

CABBAGE DELIGHT

Enough for 4 to 6

**1 small onion and/or green
  pepper**
50 g/2 oz butter
1 small firm cabbage
Salt and freshly ground pepper

1. Peel and finely slice the onion.
Slice the pepper finely, discarding core
and seeds.
2. Put these in a large bowl, add the
butter. Cover and cook on full power
for 5 minutes.
3. Meanwhile, slice the cabbage,
removing any large pieces of stalk.
4. Add the cabbage to the onion and
pepper and toss gently to mix.
5. Cover again and cook on full power
for a further 10 minutes. Stir halfway
to ensure even cooking. Precise timing
depends on size of cabbage, which is
usually cooked 7 to 8 minutes to
450 g/1 lb.
6. Add seasoning to taste.

Sybil Norcott
Irlam, Nr Manchester

SPICY CABBAGE WITH COCONUT

This dish would normally be stir-fried
on top of the stove. It is perfect for the
microwave cooker. The cabbage
remains a brilliant green, the smell of
spices does not pervade the house and
it is very quick to make.

Serves 4

**225 g/$\frac{1}{2}$ lb spring greens, cabbage
  or Chinese leaves, finely-
  shredded as for coleslaw**
$\frac{1}{2}$ medium-sized onion, chopped
2 cloves of garlic, crushed
$\frac{1}{2}$ teaspoon ground cumin
$\frac{1}{2}$ teaspoon ground coriander
$\frac{1}{4}$ teaspoon turmeric
1 teaspoon salt
**2 tablespoons unsweetened
  desiccated coconut**
**1 or 2 green chillis, finely-
  chopped**
3 tablespoons water

1. In a large (2.75 litre/4$\frac{1}{2}$ to 5 pint)
bowl mix all the ingredients
thoroughly.
2. Cover and cook on full power for 4
to 5 minutes. Stir halfway through
cooking.

Priya Wickramasinghe
Cardiff

BUTTERED CARROTS AND THYME

Serves 2

225 g/8 oz small carrots
3 tablespoons water
15 g/$\frac{1}{2}$ oz butter
1 teaspoon chopped fresh thyme

1. Trim carrots and gently scrub
clean, leaving skin on. Cut into
matchstick strips (known as julienne).
2. Put the water and carrots in a
medium-sized (2 litre/3$\frac{1}{2}$ pint) bowl.
Cook covered on full power for 5 to 6
minutes or until nearly tender. Stir
halfway through cooking. Leave to
stand covered for 4 minutes. Drain.
3. Toss in butter, sprinkle with thyme
and serve at once.

Janet Horsley
Headingley, Yorkshire

Cauliflower can be cooked whole.
Choose one of medium size, cut out the
core, stand it in a deep dish, add 2
tablespoons cold water. Cover and
cook on full power for 10 minutes. Let
it stand covered for 4 minutes before
serving.

Joan Tyers

CAULIFLOWER AND TOMATOES

Exceptionally good cooked by
microwave. The flavours remain
distinct and the tomatoes keep their

shape and colour. No difficult pans to wash. The dish is finished off under the grill.

It is good to serve on its own, but don't overcook the cauliflower. If you think 'flower' will be cooked before stalks are tender, split stalks as you do with Brussels sprouts.

Serves 3 to 4

1 medium-sized cauliflower
4 tablespoons water
1 onion
1 clove of garlic (optional)
450 g/1 lb tomatoes, or a 400 g/ 14 oz can
½ tablespoon oil
25 g/1 oz butter
1 tablespoon chopped parsley
Black pepper

Sauce

40 g/1½ oz margarine
40 g/1½ oz flour
300 ml/½ pint milk
125 g/4 oz grated cheese
25 g/1 oz dried or fresh breadcrumbs

1. Divide cauliflower into even-sized florets and put them in a large bowl with 4 tablespoons water.
2. Cook covered on full power for 7 to 8 minutes. Stir halfway through cooking.
3. Drain off cauliflower water into a cup for later use and keep cauliflower warm.
4. Meanwhile, peel and chop onion. Crush garlic.
5. Skin the tomatoes (*see Aubergines and Tomatoes page 56, paragraph 1*) and cut into quarters.
6. Put the oil and butter into the heatproof casserole in which the dish will be served. Add the onion and garlic. Cook covered on full power for 3 minutes or until onion is soft.
7. Add tomatoes, parsley, salt and black pepper and cook 2 minutes.
8. **Now make the sauce.** Put the margarine in a 1 litre/1¾ pint jug. Cook uncovered for 1 minute.
9. Stir in the flour.

10. Make up cauliflower water with a little extra milk, if necessary, to 150 ml/¼ pint. Gradually mix this and the 300 ml/½ pint milk into sauce.
11. Cook uncovered for 4 minutes. Stir every minute to avoid lumps.
12. Add 75 g/3 oz of the cheese. Stir until melted.
13. Lay florets of cauliflower on top of tomatoes in casserole, then pour the sauce over.
14. Mix the breadcrumbs with rest of the cheese, and sprinkle on top.
15. Put dish under grill until golden-brown. Serve at once.

If cauliflower and tomato mixture need reheating, before adding sauce return casserole covered to microwave and cook on full power for 1 to 2 minutes.

The whole dish may be prepared in advance and reheated uncovered on full power for 4 to 6 minutes.

Mary Watts

A tip

Corn-on-the-cob can be cooked inside its own leafy cover. Wrap in paper towel. Cook on full power: 2 minutes for one; 4 to 5 minutes for two; 6 to 7 minutes for three; 8 to 10 minutes for four. Then wrap them in foil and leave for 5 minutes. Strip off leaves and silky strands to serve as usual.

Joan Tyers

BRAISED CELERY AND BACON

Serves 4

1 small head of celery
15 g/½ oz butter or margarine
Black pepper
½ level teaspoon nutmeg
300 ml/½ pint chicken stock
2 to 3 rashers streaky bacon

To make a meal of this, add 225 g/½ lb potatoes, peeled and cut into 1 cm/½ inch cubes, when cooking the celery at paragraph 3. No extra time is needed.

1. Wash and trim celery and cut it into strips 2.5 to 5 cm/1 to 2 inches long and about 1 cm/½ inch wide.
2. Use the butter or margarine to grease a deep casserole dish.
3. Put the celery, pepper and nutmeg in the dish. Pour over the chicken stock.
4. Cook covered on full power for 8 minutes. Stir halfway through cooking. Let it stand, covered, while frying the bacon.
5. Cut the bacon into thin strips and fry conventionally until cooked, then lay the strips over the celery.

Grace Mulligan

To melt butter straight from refrigerator: 25 g/1 oz full power, uncovered, 35 to 40 seconds; 50 g/2 oz, 45 to 50 seconds. Spitting occurs when it is overheated.

Joan Tyers

COURGETTES

A vegetable with a lovely appearance, but so delicate a taste that it needs some other flavour with it. Takes only minutes to prepare.

Serves 4

450 g/1 lb courgettes, do not peel
25 g/1 oz butter
Half a clove of garlic, crushed
Salt and black pepper

1. Wash courgettes, trim off the stalks and cut into even-sized fine rings. This can be done quickly on the mandolin cutter of a grater.
2. Put the butter and garlic in a medium-sized (2 litre/3½ pint) bowl.

Cover and cook on full power for 1 minute.
3. Add courgettes, cover and cook for 6 minutes. Stir halfway through cooking. If very finely sliced, 2 to 3 minutes may be enough.
4. Season with a little salt and plenty of freshly-ground black pepper.

Serve at once while the slices are still a brilliant green.

Mary Watts

MARROW RINGS STUFFED WITH CHICKEN AND MUSHROOMS

Serves 4

1 small marrow
1 small onion
½ green pepper
1 tablespoon cooking oil
125 g/4 oz cooked chicken
125 g/4 oz mushrooms
2 tomatoes
125 g/4 oz sweetcorn (optional)
125 g/4 oz peas (optional)
300 ml/½ pint chicken stock
1 dessertspoon cornflour
Pepper and salt
15 g/½ oz butter or margarine
Small sprigs of parsley

1. Cut marrow into 4 thick rings. Peel and remove seeds.
2. Put rings into a casserole dish.
3. Peel onion and chop finely. Slice green pepper, discarding core and seeds.
4. Put the onion, pepper and oil in a medium-sized (2 litre/3½ pint) bowl. Cover and cook on full power for 5 minutes.
5. Cut chicken into small pieces; chop mushrooms. Cut four slices of tomato and keep them for decoration, chop the rest.
6. Add chicken, mushrooms, tomatoes, sweetcorn and peas to bowl. Cook covered for 4 minutes.
7. Mix cornflour with a tablespoon of the stock. Add to the rest of the stock and pour this into chicken mixture.

Add salt and pepper if necessary. Cook uncovered for 3 minutes. Stir every minute to avoid lumps as it thickens.

8. Fill each marrow ring with the mixture. Cover. Cook on full power for 10 minutes.

9. Lay a slice of tomato on each marrow ring and dot with butter or margarine. Cook uncovered for 2 minutes.

10. Serve with a sprig of parsley on each portion.

Mrs Phyllis E. Roche,
Normanton, West Yorkshire

For a mushroom filling for pancakes, see Savoury Fillings for Pancakes, page 54

Mushrooms. Wash and dry. Put in a bowl with a nut of butter. Cover and cook on full power: 3 minutes for 100 g/4 oz.

Joan Tyers

ONION TART

Serves 4

Pastry Case

100 g/4 oz plain white flour or a mixture of white and wholewheat
50 g/2oz margarine
Pinch of salt
Cold water to mix

Filling

2 medium-sized onions, thinly-sliced
25 g/1 oz margarine or butter
50 g/2 oz grated cheese
2 lightly-beaten eggs
Salt and pepper
1 teaspoon plain flour

Milk to make up to 200 ml/7 fl oz when mixed with beaten egg
A sprinkle of paprika (optional)

1. Lightly grease a shallow 20 cm/ 8 inch pie plate or quiche dish.

2. Sift the flour and salt into a mixing bowl, rub in the margarine to the consistency of fine breadcrumbs. Mix to a light paste with a little cold water.

3. Roll out pastry on a floured board and fit into the greased dish, pressing onto the sides and base. Prick both sides and base with a fork.

4. Cook on full power for 3 minutes. Leave on one side.

5. **For the filling:** put the onions and butter in a medium-sized (2 litre/3½ pint) bowl. Cook covered for 4 minutes or until the onions are tender. Put in tart case and sprinkle over half of the grated cheese.

6. Lightly beat the eggs, salt and pepper in a measuring jug.

7. Stir the teaspoonful of flour into a little milk, add to the eggs and make the quantity up to 200 ml/7 fl oz with additional milk. Beat together.

8. Cook uncovered for 2 minutes, stirring at intervals of half a minute. Pour over the onions and cheese in the pastry case.

9. Cook uncovered on full power for 3 minutes.

10. Sprinkle remaining grated cheese on top and brown under a preheated conventional grill.

11. Sprinkle a little paprika over top of tart before serving.

Bunty Johnson
Knutsford, Cheshire

GLAZED PARSNIPS

A delicious recipe, cooked and served in the same dish. Nice with pork or poultry.

Serves 4 to 6

700 g/1½ lb parsnips
1 tablespoon brown sugar
40 g/1½ oz butter
2 teaspoons lemon juice
Juice of 1 orange (or 4 tablespoons cider)
½ teaspoon salt (optional)

1. Scrub the parsnips, or peel them, and slice into 7 mm/$\frac{1}{4}$ inch rings.
2. Put them in a shallow dish and add the sugar, butter and juices.
3. Cover and cook on full power for 9 minutes. If you prefer a crunchy texture cook only for 7 minutes. Stir halfway through cooking.
4. Leave to stand, covered, for 3 minutes before serving. Add salt if necessary.

Sybil Norcott
Irlam, Nr Manchester

SAVOURY PEANUT LOAF

Particularly quick and easy if you have a food processor. Nice hot or cold. If hot, serve with a well-flavoured tomato sauce (*see Cannelloni, page 46*). Good for picnics and packed lunches.

Serves 3 to 4

125 g/4 oz carrot, grated
125 g/4 oz celery, finely-chopped
3 tablespoons water
175 g/6 oz peanuts, chopped
  small or coarsely-ground
75 g/3 oz fresh wholewheat
  breadcrumbs
2 beaten eggs
1 tablespoon milk
2 teaspoons tomato purée
2 teaspoons mixed herbs
Pepper and salt

To Finish

25 g/1 oz butter

1. Put the carrot and celery in a medium-sized (2 litre/3½ pint) bowl with the water. Cook covered for 5 minutes.
2. Mix in remaining ingredients.
3. Lay a piece of greaseproof paper in the bottom of a greased 450 g/1 lb loaf-shaped microwave container.
4. Spoon mixture into container and press it down lightly. Dot with butter.
5. Place off-centre on a trivet or upturned plate or pie dish. Cook uncovered for 4 minutes on full power.

6. Reduce to defrost (30%) setting. Cook for 15 minutes.

Janet Horsley
Headingley, Yorkshire

CREAMED POTATOES

450 g/1 lb potatoes
2 tablespoons milk
15 g/½ oz butter

1. Peel potatoes and cut them into 2.5 cm/1 inch cubes.
2. Put them in a bowl with milk and butter.
3. Cover and cook on full power for 8 minutes. Then leave them to stand for 2 minutes.
4. Mash in the usual way.

If cooking larger quantities of potato, add at paragraph 2 the amount of milk and butter you normally use when mashing potatoes cooked in the conventional way. Allow 8 minutes per 450 g/1 lb.

Joan Tyers
South Milford, West Yorkshire

NEW POTATOES

This is a tasty dish but it takes much more time than cooking in a saucepan on the stove.

Served in a sweet glaze.

450 g/1 lb new potatoes
3 tablespoons cold water
25 g/1 oz butter
25 g/1 oz sugar

1. Put the potatoes in their jackets, and the water, into a large (2.75 litre/4½ to 5 pint) bowl. Cover and cook on full power for 9 minutes. Set aside and leave to stand covered for 8 to 10 minutes. The potatoes continue to cook during this time.
2. In a medium-sized (2 litre/3½ pint) bowl put the butter and sugar. Cook uncovered for 2 minutes, or until golden.
3. Put in potatoes with or without skins. Turn them over in glaze until they are coated and light brown.

Nice with cold ham and a green crisp salad.

Grace Mulligan

SCALLOPED NEW OR OLD POTATOES

An ideal dish for the microwave. Can also be a vegetarian dish, if the ham is replaced with celery and the larger amounts of cheese are used.

Can be made with old potatoes, but choose really waxy ones like Desirée or Dr Mackintosh.

450 g/1 lb new potatoes, scrubbed not peeled
3 tablespoons water
125 g/4 oz mushrooms, chopped
15 g/½ oz butter
125 g/4 oz cooked ham, cut in small pieces, or 125 g/4 oz celery, sliced finely
Freshly-ground black pepper

Cheese Sauce

50 g/2 oz butter
50 g/2 oz flour
1 teaspoon made mustard
A grating of nutmeg
600 ml/1 pint milk
50 to 75 g/2 to 3 oz grated cheese

Topping (optional)

25 g/1 oz fresh wholewheat or white breadcrumbs
25 to 50 g/1 to 2 oz grated cheese

1. Put potatoes (skins on) and water in a large (2.75 litre/4½ to 5 pint) bowl. Cover and cook on full power for 9 minutes. Set aside to stand, covered, for 8 to 10 minutes. Drain and slice. If using celery add it after potatoes have cooked for 5 minutes.
2. **Meanwhile make the sauce.** Put the butter in a very large (2 litre/3½ pint) jug. Cook uncovered on full power for 1 minute.
3. Stir in the flour. Gradually mix in the mustard, nutmeg and milk.
4. Cook uncovered for 6 to 8 minutes until the sauce boils. Stir after 2, 3 and 4 minutes to avoid lumps. It may take the full 8 minutes if milk is very cold.
5. Beat in the cheese. Set aside.
6. Put mushrooms and the 15 g/½ oz butter in a 600 ml/1 pint jug. Cook uncovered for 2 to 3 minutes until tender.

64

7. Arrange slices of potato overlapping in a buttered, shallow, heat-proof dish.
8. Cover with mushrooms and ham or celery. Give it a good grating of black pepper.
9. Pour over the cheese sauce.
10. **For the topping,** mix crumbs and cheese and sprinkle over the top.
11. Brown under a preheated conventional grill.

Grace Mulligan

SPINACH WITH CREAM

Spinach cooked by microwave keeps a lovely colour.

Serves 3 to 4

1 kg/2 lb fresh spinach
25 g/1 oz butter or margarine
3 to 4 tablespoons fresh breadcrumbs
2 to 3 tablespoons single cream
A good grating of whole nutmeg
Pepper and salt

1. Trim and wash spinach. Put in a large (2.75 litre/4½ to 5 pint) bowl with no extra water. Cook, covered, on full power for 5 minutes. Stir halfway through cooking.
2. Meanwhile, heat butter or margarine in a frying pan and fry breadcrumbs till golden, stirring often.
3. Drain spinach, chop, drain again and squeeze out moisture.
4. Mix in cream, nutmeg, pepper and a little salt. Put in a warmed dish and sprinkle piping hot breadcrumbs on top.

Serve at once.

Mrs Joyce Langley
Shoreham-by-Sea, West Sussex

BAKED STUFFED TOMATOES

Preparation time can be saved by using a food processor, but this dish is very quick and ideal for the microwave.

Serves 2 – a substantial dish

4 large tomatoes
1 tablespoon grated onion
100 g/4 oz grated cheese
1 thick slice wholemeal or white
  bread made into crumbs
50 g/2 oz chopped mushrooms
  (optional)
Salt and pepper
2 rashers of bacon

1. Stand tomatoes stalk end down,
slice off rounded end and scoop out
flesh with a teaspoon.
2. Mix tomato pulp with onion,
cheese, breadcrumbs, mushrooms and
seasoning. This forms a crumbly
mixture.
3. Fill tomato shells, replace the tops.
4. Spread remaining mixture in a
small greased dish. Make 4 hollows in
mixture and stand tomatoes in them.
5. Remove rinds from bacon. Cut
rashers in halves. Stretch each piece
on a board with back of a knife and
make it into a roll.
6. Thread bacon rolls on wooden
cocktail sticks. Lay these across
tomatoes.
7. Cook uncovered on full power for 5
minutes. Let dish stand for 1 minute
before serving.
8. Remove sticks from bacon rolls
before serving.

Margaret Heywood
Mankinholes, Nr Todmorden,
Lancashire

'STIR-FRY' VEGETABLES WITH BEANSPROUTS

Not strictly correct to call this a Stir-
Fry because the microwave cannot fry.
However, this dish, originally cooked
in a wok, or large frying pan, is done
beautifully by microwave.

*Served with brown rice or
wholewheat pasta makes an
appetizing light meal for 4 people*

2 tablespoons oil, sesame oil is
  best
1 onion, cut into rings
A clove of garlic, crushed
½ to 1 teaspoon ground ginger, *or*
  1 small teaspoon chopped fresh
  ginger

1 green pepper, thinly-sliced
1 large carrot, scrubbed and
  thinly-sliced
1 leek, sliced
125 g/4 oz small button
  mushrooms
150 ml/¼ pint hot water
1 to 2 tablespoons white wine
  (optional)
1 to 2 teaspoons soya sauce
225 g/8 oz beansprouts

1. Put the oil, onion, garlic and ginger
in a large (2.75 litre/4½ to 5 pint) bowl.
Cook covered on full power for 2
minutes, or until the onions are
softening.
2. Stir in the pepper, carrots and
leeks. Cook covered for 4 minutes –
stir halfway through cooking.
3. Stir in the mushrooms, water, wine
and soya sauce and lay beansprouts on
top. Cook covered for 3 to 4 minutes.
Stir halfway through cooking.

Janet Horsley
Headingley, Yorkshire

VEGETABLE HOT POT

This uses the same ingredients as
ratatouille.

Ratatouille, cooked conventionally,
takes a long time. It is very successful
in the microwave. The flavours are
good and colours attractive.

Serves 4

3 large onions
1 small green pepper
1 good-sized aubergine
450 g/1 lb ripe tomatoes or a
  400 g/14 oz can of tomatoes
1 clove of garlic
4 tablespoons cooking oil
1 teaspoon sugar
Salt
1 bay leaf and/or ½ teaspoon
  basil
Black pepper

1. Cut the onions into chunks. Cut
the green pepper into very small pieces
and the aubergine into 1 to 2 cm/½ to 1
inch cubes. Skin and roughly chop the
tomatoes. Crush the garlic.

2. Put the oil, garlic, onions, pepper and aubergine in a large bowl. Cook covered on full power for 13 minutes, or until onion is tender.
3. Add the remaining ingredients. Cover and cook for 10 minutes. Stir halfway through.

Serve with rice or pasta or even large chunks of crusty bread. Particularly good with an omelette or a cheese soufflé. Reheats well.

Mary Watts

A tip

Vegetable platter. Two or three fresh vegetables can be cooked together decoratively in a flat serving dish – e.g., sliced courgettes in centre, surrounded by a ring of finely-sliced carrots with an outer ring of cauliflower florets. Weigh the prepared vegetables, arrange them in a shallow round dish, with those that take longer to cook in the outer rings. Add 2 tablespoons water. Cover dish. Cook on full power for the time per 450 g/1 lb required by the longer cooking vegetable – e.g., if combined weight of vegetables is 675 g/1½ lb and carrots are the vegetable needing longer time, cook dish as if for 675 g/ 1½ lb carrots. Allow to stand covered for one third of the cooking time before serving.

Joan Tyers

BOILED RICE

Although no time is saved in cooking rice by microwave compared with cooking it in a saucepan on the stove, the result is good. During the standing time, the microwave can be used for a sauce (*see Liver Ragoût page 51*).

Serves 4

225 g/8 oz long grain rice
750 ml/1¼ pint boiling water or stock
A pinch of salt
¼ teaspoon cooking oil

1. Place rice in a large (2.75 litre/4½ to 5 pint) bowl. Stir in the boiling water or stock, salt and oil.
2. Cover and cook on full power for 13 minutes. Stir halfway through cooking. If using long grain brown rice, cook 5 minutes longer. The large grain brown rice will take 25 to 30 minutes.
3. Set aside, leave cover in position. Allow to stand for 10 minutes before serving. Fluff with a fork. Brown rice may require draining before serving.

To Reheat 225 g/8 oz Frozen Rice

Cover and cook for about 9 minutes on full power. Break up with a fork and gently stir after 3 and 6 minutes.

Marie Emmerson

SPAGHETTI

A pinch of salt
1 tablespoon cooking oil
1.75 litres/3 pints boiling water or stock
225 g/8 oz spaghetti, wholewheat or white

Serves 3 to 4

1. Put the salt, oil and water or stock in a large bowl. Stand the spaghetti in the water. Cook uncovered on full power for 1 to 1½ minutes.
2. Gently push the unsoftened spaghetti into the water. Cover. Cook on full power: 8 minutes for wholewheat, 6 minutes for white. Check during cooking that the spaghetti is immersed.
3. Set aside, leaving cover on for 10 minutes. Drain and serve.

Marie Emmerson

To Re-heat Frozen Spaghetti

Cooked pasta freezes quite satisfactorily in a bag. It can then be thawed and heated without removing from bag.

For 450 g/1 lb cooked frozen pasta: open the bag and put it in microwave cooker on defrost (30%) setting for 4 to 5 minutes. Reheat for 2 minutes on full power, either in the bag or in a ring around serving dish, covered in the usual way.

Joan Tyers
South Milford, West Yorkshire

MIXED 'FRIED' NOODLES, INDONESIAN-STYLE

Made with chicken and prawns. Normally cooked in a wok or a large frying pan, this dish looks and tastes good made in the microwave cooker, although nothing is fried.

Serves 4

225 g/8 oz egg noodles
1.75 litres/3 pints boiling water
2 tablespoons vegetable oil
Half a medium-sized onion, finely-chopped
2 cloves of garlic, finely-chopped
125 g/4 oz uncooked chicken flesh, cut into very small pieces
1 stick of celery, finely-chopped
50 g/2 oz Chinese cabbage, sliced
125 g/4 oz prawns, shelled
½ teaspoon salt
1 tablespoon soya sauce

To garnish

3 spring onions, sliced
Half a cucumber, finely-sliced
1 tablespoon onion flakes (can be bought at oriental food shops)

1. Put the noodles, boiling water and 1 tablespoon oil in a large (2.75 litre/4½ to 5 pint) bowl. Cook covered for 8 minutes. Set aside covered for 10 minutes.
2. Meanwhile, in another bowl, put 1 tablespoon oil, the onion and garlic. Cook covered for 2 minutes. Add the chicken. Cook for a further 3 minutes, or until chicken is cooked.
3. Add the celery and cabbage and cook for 2 minutes.

4. Drain noodles and add them with the prawns and salt and mix thoroughly.
5. Lastly, add soya sauce and cook for a further minute or so until the dish is heated through.
6. Serve in 4 shallow bowls and garnish with spring onion, cucumber and fried onion flakes.

Priya Wickramasinghe
Cardiff

QUICK PIZZA

The base is cooked in a frying pan on top of stove, the filling is made in the microwave cooker and the pizza is completed under the grill.

Enough for 3 or 4

Base

125 g/4 oz self-raising flour, wholewheat or white
¼ teaspoon salt
3 tablespoons oil
A little cold water

Filling

15 g/½ oz butter
1 small onion, finely-chopped
225 g/8 oz canned or fresh tomatoes, skinned and chopped
1 teaspoon mixed herbs

To finish

125 g/4 oz grated cheese
2 or 3 rashers of streaky bacon cut in strips, *or* anchovies soaked for 10 minutes in a little milk to remove excess salt, *or* olives

1. Mix together flour and salt. Stir in 1 tablespoon of the oil and enough water to make a fairly stiff but pliable dough.
2. Using a floured board, roll dough out to fit a frying pan, about 18 cm/ 7 inches in diameter.
3. Heat rest of oil in the pan and cook dough over moderate heat for about 5 to 6 minutes.

4. Turn it over and cook 4 to 5 minutes on the other side.

5. Meanwhile, make filling. Put the butter and onion in a 1 litre/1¾ pint jug. Cover and cook on full power for 3 minutes, or until onion is soft.

6. Add tomatoes and herbs and cook on full power for 2 minutes. Drain off excess liquid.

7. Spread tomato mixture on top of cooked pizza base in pan.

8. Sprinkle with cheese.

9. If using bacon, arrange the strips on top of cheese and put under a moderate grill for a few minutes. If using anchovies, pat dry, arrange on top of cheese and grill. If using olives, use them to decorate after cheese has melted under grill.

Grace Mulligan

Long Mezières Leek.

Chapter 6

Sauces, Savoury and Sweet

Some extra useful information, but not necessary for following the recipes.

Sauces are simple to make in the microwave cooker and have the advantage that sticking, scorching and burning do not occur. Use a jug large enough to accommodate the sauce when it bubbles up to boiling point. 300 ml/½ pint of sauce will take about 4 minutes, uncovered, on full power to cook and it is advisable to stir every minute to avoid lumps. **Egg-based sauces,** *such as Bearnaise and custards, need close attention and should be checked every 15 to 30 seconds to avoid curdling, but if the instructions are followed carefully you will find it easier by microwave.*

Thawing and heating

The container needs to be large enough to avoid boiling over and generally the full power setting can be used. The time to thaw and heat will depend upon the ingredients and consistency of the sauce, but allow about 7 minutes for 300 ml/½ pint. About halfway through, break the sauce up to speed the process. At the completion of thawing and heating, whisk the sauce if the consistency is not smooth.

BASIC WHITE SAUCES

40 g/1½ oz butter or margarine
40 g/1½ oz plain flour
Salt and pepper

Thick Sauce

300 ml/½ pint milk or stock

Medium thick

450 ml/¾ pint milk or stock

Thin

600 ml/1 pint milk or stock

1. Put the butter in a 1 litre/1¾ pint jug. Cook uncovered on full power for 1 minute, or until melted. Stir in the flour.
2. Gradually mix in the milk or stock.

Cook uncovered as follows:
Thick sauce – approximately 4 minutes
Medium thick sauce – approximately 6 minutes
Thin sauce – approximately 7 minutes
Stir frequently to avoid lumps. The sauce should come to the boil and cook for 30 seconds. Timings vary according to how cold the milk is.
3. Season to taste.

All-in-one method preferred by Grace Mulligan, who likes to use a very large (2 litre/3½ pint) jug and a coil whisk. A balloon whisk will do the job also.

1. Whisk the butter, flour and milk together in the jug. It does not matter

if the butter does not combine at this stage.

2. Cook on full power for three 2-minute bursts, whisking very thoroughly between each burst. Season to taste.

Savoury Sauces

Anchovy
Anchovies pounded to a purée and added at the last minute to white sauce, made with milk or stock as above. Quantity of anchovies to your taste. Reheat uncovered on full power for 1 minute.

Cheese
50 to 75 g/2 to 3 oz grated, hard, well-flavoured cheese added after cooking the sauce, which will be hot enough to melt it. Reheating is as a rule unnecessary.

Egg
1 or 2 hard-boiled eggs, chopped small, added at last minute to medium thick or thin sauce made with milk, as above. Do **NOT** attempt to boil eggs in the microwave cooker.

Parsley
Medium thick white sauce made with milk or stock as above, adding plenty of chopped fresh parsley at the last minute until sauce is nearly green.

Tomato
Using medium thick or thin white sauce made as above with stock. Remove pan from heat and stir in tomato purée, thyme or basil to taste and a pinch of sugar.

Sweet Sauces

Coffee
Make up thin sauce as above with half milk and half strong coffee. Add sugar to taste – but no salt and pepper!

Vanilla
Make up thin white sauce as above, using milk (and no salt or pepper!). Add a vanilla pod while sauce is simmering. Then remove it, wash and dry and store for further use.

Grace Mulligan

A tip

Cleaning the microwave cooker. Wipe over regularly with a damp, soapy cloth. For congealed fat, bring a small container of water to the boil on full power. The steam will soften it so that it can be cleaned easily.

Joan Tyers

BÉCHAMEL SAUCE

A gently-flavoured classic white sauce.

300 ml/½ pint milk
½ bay leaf
2 peppercorns
1 blade of mace
A piece of carrot, 5 cm/2 inches
¼ of a medium-sized onion
25 g/1 oz butter
25 g/1 oz flour
Salt and pepper

1. Put the milk, bay leaf, peppercorns, mace, carrot and onion in a medium-sized (2 litre/3½ pint) jug or bowl. Cook uncovered on full power for 3 minutes.
2. Leave to infuse for 10 minutes before straining. Discard the spices and vegetables.
3. Put the butter in a 1 litre/1¾ pint jug and cook on full power for 1 minute, or until melted.
4. Stir in the flour. Gradually mix in the milk. Cook for 2½ minutes until thick and smooth. Stir every minute to avoid lumps.
5. Season to taste.

Grace Mulligan

BREAD SAUCE

1 medium-sized onion
2 cloves
450 ml/¾ pint milk
½ level teaspoon salt
6 peppercorns
A small piece of bay leaf

175 to 200 g/6 to 7 oz fresh
   wholemeal or white
   breadcrumbs
15 g/½ oz butter

1. Peel onion. Stick the cloves into it.
2. Put the onion, milk, salt,
peppercorns and bayleaf in a very
large (2 litre/3½ pint) jug. Cook
uncovered for 5 minutes.
3. Remove from heat and set aside for
30 minutes or longer.
4. Strain milk. Cook uncovered for 3
minutes. Pour over the crumbs, add
butter and stir.
5. Pour into a heat-proof dish. Cover.
Cook for 5 minutes. Stir halfway
through cooking.

Grace Mulligan

CURRY SAUCE

A useful sauce which can be stored in
the freezer ready to take out for a
quick meal.

300 ml/½ pint light stock
1 heaped tablespoon coconut
25 g/1 oz butter or good dripping
1 finely-chopped onion
1 thinly-sliced apple
1 level tablespoon curry powder
1 level tablespoon plain flour
1 tablespoon sultanas
1 tablespoon chutney
1 dessertspoon brown sugar
1 dessertspoon lemon juice

1. Put stock in a 600 ml/1 pint jug.
Cook uncovered on full power for 4
minutes, or until boiling.
2. Pour stock over the coconut. Leave
to infuse for 10 to 15 minutes. Strain
stock, discard coconut.
3. Put the fat, onion and apple in a 1
litre/1¾ pint jug. Cover and cook for 2
minutes on full power. Stir in curry
powder and flour. Cook uncovered for
1 minute.
4. Stir in the stock. Cook uncovered
for 4 minutes. Stir every minute.
5. Add remaining ingredients. Cook
uncovered on full power for 2 minutes.

Reduce to defrost (30%) setting and
cook for 15 minutes.

If becoming too thick, add a little more
stock, but the sauce should not be
thin.

Serve over hot, hard-boiled eggs. Or
add cooked meat and vegetables
towards end of cooking time, making
sure these are thoroughly heated
through before serving.

Dorothy Sleightholme

A tip

Smells. If you cannot remove a smell
by wiping the cooker with a hot damp
cloth and a spot of detergent: put a
piece of lemon rind or a dash of lemon
juice (bottled variety is suitable) into a
small bowl with 300 ml/½ pint water
and let it boil uncovered in the
microwave cooker on full power for 1
to 2 minutes. Then wipe with a clean
tea towel.

Joan Tyers

TO MAKE GRAVY

1 tablespoon dripping or meat
   juices
2 tablespoons plain flour,
   wholewheat or white
600 ml/1 pint hot meat or
   vegetable stock
A little gravy browning
Salt and pepper

1. Put the dripping or meat juices in a
1 litre/1¾ pint jug. Blend in the flour.
Gradually add the stock and gravy
browning.
2. Cook uncovered on full power 4 to 5
minutes. Stir every minute to avoid
lumps. Add salt and pepper to taste.

A PIQUANT PARSLEY SAUCE

25 g/1 oz butter
25 g/1 oz flour
Salt and pepper
300 ml/½ pint milk
1 teaspoon lemon juice
A nut of butter
2 tablespoons freshly-chopped
  parsley

1. Put butter in a 600 ml/1 pint jug.
Cook uncovered on full power for 1
minute, or until melted.
2. Stir in the flour, salt and pepper.
Gradually mix in the milk. Cook
uncovered for 4 minutes. Stir every
minute to avoid lumps.
3. Beat in lemon juice and a nut of
butter. Stir in lots of parsley.

Dorothy Sleightholme

A SWEET AND SOUR SAUCE

For breast of lamb, but also good with
sausages, belly pork, pork chops and
spare ribs. This kind of sauce is
excellent for the microwave cooker
compared with a saucepan on top of
the stove, where it can easily burn.

50 g/2 oz chopped pineapple, or 2
  tablespoons pineapple jam
50 g/2 oz finely-chopped onion
1 tablespoon vinegar
1 heaped tablespoon sugar
½ tablespoon tomato purée or
  ketchup
1 dessertspoon cornflour
2 teaspoons soya sauce
300 ml/½ pint water
2 teaspoons oil

1. Prepare pineapple and onion and
put it in a small bowl. Cook covered on
full power for 3 minutes. Set aside.
2. Blend together in a 600 ml/1 pint
jug the vinegar, sugar, tomato purée,
cornflour, soya sauce and stir in the
water.
3. Cook uncovered on full power for 4
minutes until thick. Stir every minute
to avoid lumps.

4. Stir in the oil, pineapple and onion
and cook for 2 minutes more.

Mrs Edith Griffiths
Buckley, Clwyd

COOKED SALAD DRESSING

A good economical dressing which
looks like mayonnaise but as it uses no
oil, does not taste so rich. The recipe is
very successful in the microwave.

Keeps for a week in a cool place. Keeps
for at least two weeks, covered, in a
refrigerator.

2 teaspoons sugar
½ level teaspoon dry mustard
¼ level teaspoon salt
25 g/1 oz margarine
2 tablespoons vinegar
1 tablespoon lemon juice
1 egg

1. Put sugar, mustard and salt in a
small (600 ml/1 pint) jug with the
margarine cut into small pieces.
2. Cook uncovered on full power for 1
minute.
3. Whisk in the vinegar and lemon
juice.
4. Whisk the egg separately, then
whisk it into mixture in jug.
5. Cook for 30 to 45 seconds, whisking
every 15 seconds until mixture coats
the back of a wooden spoon. It will
thicken well, but be very careful not to
overheat.
6. Allow to cool.

Margaret Heywood
Mankinholes, Nr Todmorden,
Lancashire

CARAMEL SAUCE

A sauce to serve either hot or cold
with ice-cream.

*Serves 4 to 6, depending on the size
of your tablespoons*

2 tablespoons golden syrup
25 g/1 oz butter
2 tablespoons water

1. Measure the golden syrup with a warm tablespoon and put it into a 600 ml/1 pint heatproof jug.
2. Cook uncovered on full power for about 1 minute or until turning brown.
3. Remove from microwave cooker and add the butter, stir well.
4. Add the water and mix well.

When served hot this sauce is very runny. As it cools it becomes thicker.

Sue Probert
Warwick

CHOCOLATE SAUCE

1 level dessertspoon cornflour
25 to 50 g/1 to 2 oz sugar
15 g/½ oz cocoa
300 ml/½ pint milk
15 g/½ oz margarine
½ teaspoon vanilla essence

1. Blend cornflour, sugar and cocoa with a little of the milk in a 1 litre/1¾ pint jug.
2. Pour the remaining milk into a 600 ml/1 pint jug. Cook uncovered on full power for 3 minutes.
3. Pour the hot milk on to the cornflour mixture. Stir well.
4. Cook uncovered for 2 to 3 minutes, or until thick. Stir every minute to avoid lumps.
5. Remove and stir in margarine and essence.

QUICK CHOCOLATE SAUCE

Best served hot or warm.

50 g/2 oz dark cooking chocolate
A small nut of butter
50 g/2 oz sugar
60 ml/2 fl oz water

1. Break the chocolate into pieces and put them into a 600 ml/1 pint jug. Cook uncovered on full power for 3 to 4 minutes, or until melted.
2. Stir in the butter, sugar and water. Cook for a further 2 to 3 minutes. Stir frequently and beat before serving.

Anne Wallace
Stewarton, Ayrshire

POURING CUSTARD

300 ml/½ pint milk
2 egg-yolks
1 tablespoon sugar

1. Put the milk, egg-yolks and sugar in a 600 ml/1 pint jug. Whisk well.
2. Cook uncovered for 3 to 4 minutes. Check and stir frequently. Cook until it thickens, but do not allow to boil. When it is thick enough the mixture will just coat the back of the spoon.

Mrs Janice Langley
Shoreham-by-Sea, West Sussex

CUSTARD SAUCE

2 level dessertspoons custard
  powder
2 level dessertspoons sugar
1 pint milk

1. Use a very large jug to prevent the custard boiling over. A coil or balloon whisk is handy.
2. Whisk all ingredients together.
3. Cook on full power for three 2-minute bursts, whisking very thoroughly between each burst.

For a thicker custard to set in a mould, or for use in a trifle, increase the custard powder to 2 rounded tablespoons.

Grace Mulligan

FUDGE SAUCE

For plain ice-cream

50 g/2 oz butter
50 g/2 oz granulated sugar
75 g/3 oz soft brown sugar
125 g/5 oz golden syrup

Place all the ingredients in a 1 litre/1¾ pint jug. Cook uncovered on full power for 4 minutes, or until the sugar has dissolved. Stir every minute and take care that it does not go too dark and burn.

Grace Mulligan

MELBA SAUCE

For puddings or ice-cream.

This sauce freezes well.

Raspberries, fresh or frozen
Icing sugar

1. Sieve uncooked raspberries to make a purée.
2. Sift icing sugar and beat it into purée, one teaspoon at a time, until sauce is sufficiently sweet.

To serve hot

Put the prepared sauce into a jug. Cook uncovered on full power until hot. One minute will be long enough for 300 ml/½ pint of sauce.

Anne Wallace
Stewarton, Ayrshire

ORANGE SAUCE FOR PANCAKES

Pancakes cannot be made in the microwave, but this sauce is very easy and makes a good substitute sauce for Crêpes Suzette. (*See Pancakes with savoury fillings, page 54 for a basic pancake recipe.*)

Enough sauce for 6 six-inch pancakes

50 g/2 oz butter
Grated rind and juice of 1 large orange
25 to 50 g/1 to 2 oz caster sugar
4 tablespoons sherry or sweet white wine

1. Lay pancakes, as they are cooked, on a clean cloth placed on a large cake wire. Then fold them in quarters and arrange in a shallow dish.
2. Put the butter in a 600 ml/1 pint jug. Cook uncovered for 1 to 1½ minutes.

3. Stir in the orange rind and juice, then sugar. Continue cooking for 1 to 1½ minutes. Stir well to dissolve sugar. Add sherry or sweet white wine.
4. Pour the sauce over the pancakes. Cook uncovered to reheat, if necessary, 2 to 3 minutes.

Dorothy Sleightholme

Juice of oranges and lemons will be easier to extract if the whole fruit is warmed for 15 seconds on full power before squeezing.

Joan Tyers

RUM SAUCE

For Christmas Pudding and also for other steamed puddings (*see page 79*).

600 ml/1 pint milk
25 g/1 oz cornflour
25 g/1 oz sugar
2 tablespoons rum, or more if desired

1. Put milk, cornflour and sugar into a very large (2 litre/3½ pint) jug. Whisk vigorously. Cook uncovered on full power for 2 minutes.
2. Whisk again, taking care to gather up any mixture in corners of jug. Cook 2 minutes more.
3. Whisk again as before, and cook a further 2 minutes.
4. Whisk in the rum.

Two tablespoonfuls of cream added with the rum is delicious. Brandy or sherry sauce can be made in exactly the same way.

Grace Mulligan

Chapter 7

Puddings, Hot and Cold

Some extra useful information, but not necessary for following the recipes.

Many puddings normally steamed for an hour or so can be cooked by microwave, and the cooking time is incredibly short. Best served freshly-made – if left to cool they tend to dehydrate and harden. Generally, the high power setting is used and the container is covered to avoid unnecessary evaporation. The container may be greased, or greased and lined with cling film or greaseproof paper. But do not flour as this will remain on the pudding when it is turned out and look disagreeable. A 2-egg **sponge pudding** *takes about 6 minutes to cook on full power and should be left to stand for about 2 to 3 minutes before turning out. A 1-egg* **suet pudding** *takes about 4 minutes to cook and is given the same standing time. Joan Tyers recommends removing the cover as soon as the pudding is taken from the cooker. Otherwise, in her experience, the cling film can contract and squash the pudding into a tough ball.*

Fruit *cooks beautifully in the microwave. Details are given on page 83.*

Puddings which contain a lot of air and need heat to achieve a set, are not successful – for example, hot soufflés. Do not attempt fried puddings such as fritters in a microwave cooker as there is no control over the temperature of the oil or fat. These should always be cooked conventionally.

Thawing and re-heating

Although 'steamed' puddings can be thawed and reheated in a microwave, Marie Emmerson believes the best result is achieved by steaming on a conventional hob for about 1 hour. Biddy Clayton reheats individual portions covered with sauce or custard for 2 minutes on full power.

APPLE AND FIG CRUMBLE

Serves 4

Crumble

50 g/2 oz butter, or 2 tablespoons
   vegetable oil
50 g/2 oz wholewheat flour
40 g/1½ oz porridge oats
15 g/½ oz desiccated coconut
Several drops of vanilla essence

Filling

125 g/4 oz figs, chopped
150 ml/¼ pint water
225 g/8 oz cooking apples,
   peeled, cored and sliced

This recipe was prepared for people trying to cut down on sugar. If you cannot manage unsweetened crumble, add 25 to 50 g/1 to 2 oz demerara sugar at paragraph 2.

1. Put butter in a 600 ml/1 pint jug and cook uncovered on full power for 30 seconds, or until melted. Watch that it does not overheat or butter will spit.
2. Mix into the other crumble ingredients.
3. Put the figs and water in a casserole dish. Cover and cook on full power for 3 minutes.
4. Mix in apples. Sprinkle crumble mixture over fruit.
5. Cook uncovered for 5 minutes. Stand for 3 minutes before serving.

Brown under a preheated grill if desired, but watch it in case it burns, especially if sugar has been added to crumble.

Janet Horsley
Headingley, Yorkshire

MALVERN APPLE PUDDING

Puddings of this kind are supremely successful in a microwave, saving at least an hour on the conventional steaming time. It is advisable to use brown sugar and brown flour, or half wholewheat and half white flour, for a good colour to the pudding.

Malvern is apple-growing country. Although this dish is made with Russet apples, small sweet eating apples can be used.

Enough for 6 but easy to make half quantity

125 g/4 oz butter
125 g/4 oz soft brown sugar
2 beaten eggs
125 g/4 oz plain or self-raising brown or wheatmeal flour
A pinch of salt
2 smallish Russet apples (about 225 g/8 oz peeled and cored)
Grated rind of 1 lemon
50 g/2 oz currants
2 to 3 tablespoons brandy

It is nearly as nice with sherry, or $\frac{1}{2}$ teaspoon brandy flavouring with 2 tablespoons of milk, or even with apple juice.

1. Cream butter and sugar together.
2. Add beaten eggs.
3. Fold in flour and salt.
4. Peel, core and chop apples and mix with lemon rind, currants and brandy.
5. Grease a 1.1 litre/2 pint pudding basin. Put a small square of greased, greaseproof paper to cover bottom of basin to help when pudding is turned out.
6. Put mixture in basin and cover loosely with cling film.
7. Cook for 6 minutes on full power. Turn basin halfway through cooking. If cooking half quantity, or two small puddings, cook each pudding separately on full power for 4 minutes.
8. Remove cover and let pudding stand for 3 minutes before serving.
9. Turn pudding out on a warmed dish and serve at once with custard, or brandy or sherry sauce.

(*See recipes for custard and rum or sherry sauce on pages 73 and 74.*)

This type of pudding should be eaten at once as it tends to go hard as it cools.

Mrs Cynthia Cooksey
Crofton Hackett, Worcestershire

BAKED BANANAS

Serves 4

4 bananas
Lemon juice
50 g/2 oz desiccated coconut
50 g/2 oz demerara sugar
Pat of butter
A little rum (optional)

1. Lay the peeled bananas in a buttered, shallow dish.
2. Sprinkle with lemon juice.
3. Mix the coconut and sugar together and sprinkle this over the bananas.
4. Add shavings of butter and a sprinkling of rum if you wish.
5. Cover dish. Cook on full power for 2 minutes. Rearrange if necessary. Cook for a further 2 minutes, but you may find the bananas are sufficiently cooked after only 2 minutes.

Serve with custard (*see page 73*) or cream.

Mary Berry

The right consistency for a microwave cake or pudding mixture: it should drop off the spoon to the count of 1-2-3. If necessary, add 2 or 3 tablespoons cold water. Too much liquid produces a heavy result.

Joan Tyers

BAKED CUSTARD

Works well in the microwave, although the surface may not be smooth.

Serves 4

3 eggs and 1 egg-yolk
1 heaped dessertspoon honey or
** 1 level tablespoon vanilla sugar**
425 ml/¾ pint milk
A grating of nutmeg

1. Lightly beat eggs and egg-yolk with the honey or sugar.
2. Pour the milk into this mixture.
3. Strain into a serving dish. Grate on fresh nutmeg.
4. Cook uncovered on defrost (30%) setting for 30 minutes, or until cooked. To test, slip a knife in diagonally. If it comes out clean, custard is cooked.

Serve hot or cold.

Mary Watts

Crumble puddings. Use wholewheat flour and/or dark brown sugar for a nice golden topping. Best of all if browned and crisped a little under the grill after cooking, but take care because it burns very easily.

Joan Tyers

PINEAPPLE PUDDING

Can also be made with stewed rhubarb or plums. To stew fruit in the microwave cooker, *see page 83*.

Serves 5 to 6

50 g/2 oz margarine
100 g/4 oz plain white flour
425 ml/¾ pint milk
50 g/2 oz sugar
A 450 g/16 oz can of pineapple
** pieces**
2 egg-yolks

Meringue

2 egg-whites
75 g/3 oz caster sugar

1. Heat grill just to warm, and put a deep 1.1 litre/2 pint dish under to warm.
2. Put the margarine in a large (1 litre/1¾ pint) jug. Cook uncovered on full power until melted. Stir in the flour. Gradually stir in the milk. Cook uncovered for 5 minutes. Stir every minute to avoid lumps.
3. Mix in sugar and 150 ml/¼ pint of juice drained from pineapple. Cook for a further 2 minutes.
4. Beat in the egg-yolks. Cook for 1 minute. Beat again.
5. Lastly, mix in pineapple pieces and pour into the warmed dish. Put back under grill to keep warm.
6. Whisk egg-whites until they stand up in peaks. Add sugar and whisk again.
7. Spread this meringue over pudding and put dish back under grill. Keep heat low. Grill for 15 minutes until top is a lovely golden brown.

This meringue is not crisp, but soft like marshmallow.

Mrs Patricia Chantry
Hook, Nr Goole, N. Humberside

PINEAPPLE UPSIDE-DOWN PUDDING

Serves 4

Base

25 g/1 oz butter

50 g/2 oz demerara sugar
4 pineapple rings
6 glacé cherries

Pudding

50 g/2 oz soft margarine
50 g/2 oz caster sugar
1 large egg
60 g/2½ oz self-raising flour
15 g/½ oz semolina
1 to 2 tablespoons milk

Glaze

1 teaspoon arrowroot or
  cornflour
150 ml/¼ pint from tin of
  pineapple (if not sufficient,
  make up with water)

1. Butter a 1.2 litre/2 pint soufflé dish
with the 25 g/1 oz butter, spreading it
lightly around sides, thicker at the
bottom. Sprinkle with the demerara
sugar. Cook uncovered on full power
for ¾ to 1 minute.
2. Arrange pineapple rings and
cherries in a pattern over base.
3. Put all pudding ingredients, except
the milk, in a mixing bowl and mix
together but do not beat hard. Add
enough of the milk to make a soft,
dropping consistency.
4. Spread carefully into the dish on
top of fruit and level the top.
5. Cook uncovered on full power for 6
minutes. Turn dish around halfway
through cooking.
6. Remove from microwave and let it
stand for 2 to 3 minutes. Invert on to a
warm plate, leaving dish in position
until ready to serve.
7. **For the glaze:** mix arrowroot and
juice in a 600 ml/1 pint jug. Cook for 2
minutes, or until boiling and
transparent. Stir every 30 seconds.
Spoon a little of the glaze over the
pudding. Serve remainder as a sauce.

Dorothy Sleightholme

QUEEN OF PUDDINGS

Very good results in the microwave
cooker. Grill or oven required to finish
meringue.

Serves 4

425 ml/¾ pint milk
25 g/1 oz butter
Rind of 1 small lemon
125 g/4 oz caster sugar
75 g/3 oz fresh white
  breadcrumbs
2 eggs, separated
50 g/2 oz (2 tablespoons) jam

1. Put the milk into a 1 litre/1¾ pint
jug. Cook uncovered for 4½ minutes on
full power until nearly boiling. Stir in
butter, finely-grated rind of lemon and
25 g/1 oz of the caster sugar.
2. Pour this over the crumbs in a bowl
and stir in egg-yolks. Leave for 15
minutes.
3. Pour into a lightly-greased 1 to 1.2
litre/1½ to 2 pint heat-proof dish, and
cook uncovered on full power for 5
minutes. Stir halfway through
cooking. Set aside to cool.
4. Put the jam in a small bowl. Cook
uncovered for 1 minute. Gently spread
over the cooked mixture and leave to
cool again.
5. Whisk egg-whites stiffly, fold in the
remaining 75 g/3 oz caster sugar and
spread on top. Sift on a little extra
caster sugar.
6. Brown under a preheated grill or
cook in a cool oven, Gas 1, 275°F,
140°C, for 20 minutes or until
meringue is set and tinged with gold.

A tip

Jam for pouring over sponge
puddings, etc. Remove metal lid, put
jar of jam into microwave cooker on
full power for 1 minute. Jam sets again
when cold.

Joan Tyers

'STEAMED' PUDDINGS

These recipes, which traditionally would be steamed for at least 1½ hours, creating steam in the kitchen, anxiety in case they boil dry and more pans to wash, are one of the miracles of the microwave. The time and effort saved makes them well worth reintroducing to family menus.

Serves 4

The basic recipe

50 g/2 oz margarine
50 g/2 oz caster sugar
75 g/3 oz self-raising flour, either
  wholewheat or white, or half
  and half
Pinch of salt
1 beaten egg
2 tablespoons milk

1. Grease a 600 ml/1 pint heat-proof basin.
2. Beat margarine until soft and creamy, then beat in sugar.
3. Mix flour and salt and add it a little at a time alternately with the beaten egg.
4. Fold in milk.
5. Spoon into greased basin, smooth top.
6. Cover loosely with cling film, tucking edges securely around rim.
7. Cook on full power for 3½ minutes. Remove cover, let pudding stand for 2 minutes before turning out.

Serve with custard or chocolate sauce or with warmed golden syrup or a jam sauce. (*See the sauces chapter, pages 69 to 74*).

Try also the following variations, based on the Steamed Pudding recipe.

Marble Pudding

When pudding is mixed:

1. Divide mixture into 3 portions.
2. Colour one portion pink, with a few drops of red colouring.
3. Mix 2 teaspoons of cocoa with 2 teaspoons of hot water. Fold this into another portion.
4. Spoon into the greased pudding basin alternate spoonfuls of the plain, pink and chocolate mixtures. Smooth top.
Continue from paragraph 6 of the basic recipe.
Serve with custard or chocolate sauce (*see page 73*).

Sultana Pudding

Follow the basic recipe, adding 50 g/2 oz sultanas to the flour (paragraph 3).

Chocolate Pudding

Omit 25 g/1 oz flour from the basic recipe and replace it with 25 g/1 oz cocoa. Sieve this with the flour and add as instructed in paragraph 3 of basic recipe.

Coffee Pudding

Dissolve 2 level teaspoons instant coffee into 2 teaspoons boiling water. Mix this with the milk and fold in as instructed in paragraph 4 of basic recipe.

Orange or Lemon Pudding

Omit the milk from the basic recipe and add the rind and juice of 1 small orange or lemon.

Jam, Marmalade, Golden Syrup or Lemon Curd may be

used as a topping for the pudding. Follow the basic recipe but put 1 to 2 tablespoons of jam, marmalade, golden syrup or curd into the greased pudding basin before spooning in the pudding mixture.

If there is some left over, this type of pudding can be frozen. Although it may become hard when left to go cold, it reheats well, especially in slices with a coating of custard or sauce.

Dorothy Sleightholme

WHITE LADIES PUDDING

This recipe is named after a village near Worcester, called White Ladies Aston, where a convent of Cistercian nuns lived in the 12th Century. They wore white habits. It would originally have been steamed for 1½ hours and more recently baked in the oven also for 1½ hours. By microwave it takes just 10 minutes to cook and saves on washing up too.

Serves 4

4 medium-thick slices of white bread
50 g/2 oz butter
75 g/3 oz desiccated coconut
425 ml/¾ pint milk
A pinch of salt
Vanilla essence
2 eggs
50 g/2 oz sugar

1. Remove crusts from bread. Butter it thickly and cut into squares or triangles.
2. Use remaining butter to grease a 1.5 litre/2½ pint pie dish. Sprinkle it with the coconut. Then arrange bread in dish.
3. Put milk in a 600 ml/1 pint jug. Cook uncovered on full power until comfortably hot when tested with little finger. Add salt and a few drops of vanilla essence.
4. Beat eggs with sugar. Pour in milk, stirring to dissolve sugar, and strain into pie dish. Leave to soak for 20 minutes.
5. Cook covered with cling film for 7 minutes. Let it stand uncovered for 3 minutes before serving.
6. Turn pudding out on to a warmed dish. Delicious hot or cold.

Mrs Jean Round
Cookley, Worcestershire

Custard powder can be used to improve the colour of cakes or puddings made with white flour. Substitute 15 g/½ oz custard powder for 15 g/½ oz of the flour.

Joan Tyers

CHOCOLATE ORANGE MOUSSE

Makes 6 individual helpings

175 g/6 oz plain cooking chocolate
1 orange
15 g/½ oz butter
3 eggs, separated
150 ml/¼ pint whipped cream
1 teaspoon caster sugar
Chopped walnuts to decorate

1. Break up chocolate and put it in a 600 ml/1 pint jug. Cook uncovered on full power for 2½ minutes, or until soft. Check and stir after 2 minutes.
2. Grate zest from orange. Squeeze out juice.
3. Stir butter, orange zest and juice into chocolate. Mix well.
4. Beat in egg-yolks one at a time.
5. Mix in whipped cream.
6. Whisk egg-whites firmly, then whisk in sugar.
7. Fold egg-whites into chocolate mixture.
8. Serve in small sundae glasses.

Decorate with a sprinkling of chopped walnuts when cool.

Dorothy Sleightholme

To reheat a pastry pie: stand it on a paper towel on a plate. Do not cover. Heat on full power. Time varies according to shape and size of pie. It is the filling which heats first, so the important thing is to test by feeling underneath the pie, not the top or sides. If the bottom is hot, remove from microwave cooker and let it stand for 2 minutes before serving, so that heat of filling reaches through pastry (and so that there are no mouths burnt on the filling). When overheated, pastry goes soft, but as it cool it goes rock hard.

Joan Tyers

CHOCOLATE SUPRÊME

Very rich. Best made the day before it is needed so that flavour matures.

Freezes well up to 3 months.

Enough for 6 to 8 people but you can make half quantity

125 g/4 oz best quality plain eating chocolate
90 g/3½ oz butter, cut in small pieces – at room temperature
4 eggs, separated
1 tablespoon brandy or very dry sherry
2 level dessertspoons icing sugar, sieved
3 tablespoons double cream
To decorate: toasted flaked almonds (*see below*) or piped double cream

1. Break up chocolate and put it in a 600 ml/1 pint jug. Cook uncovered on full power for 2 minutes, or until soft. Check and stir after 1½ minutes.
2. Meanwhile, prepare butter. If it is straight from refrigerator, cut it in small pieces, arrange on a plate and put in microwave on full power for 10 seconds. It needs to be added to dish at room temperature but do not let it melt in microwave.
3. Add egg-yolks to melted chocolate and mix gently. Do not beat at any stage in this recipe.
4. Add the small pieces of butter and stir gently until dissolved.
5. Now add brandy or sherry and sieved icing sugar. Stir until dissolved.

6. Lastly, add cream and stir again.
7. In another bowl, whisk egg-whites until thick and fluffy and fold into chocolate mixture.
8. Pour into tiny glasses, cover with foil or cling film and keep in refrigerator until needed.
9. Just before serving, decorate with a sprinkling of toasted almonds or a whirl of double cream.

Grace Mulligan

CHRISTMAS JELLY

Made in a pudding basin so that the jelly looks like a Christmas pudding.

Serves 4 to 6

450 g/1 lb black grapes
1½ packets of dark jelly (blackcurrant or blackberry)
150 ml/¼ pint port or sherry
Water
50 g/2 oz raisins
50 g/2 oz chopped blanched almonds*

* *To blanch almonds: put them in a basin, pour over boiling water to cover. Leave until cool enough to handle, when almonds will squeeze easily out of their skins.*

1. Wash grapes and dry carefully. Cut each grape in half and remove seeds.

2. Cut the jelly into pieces and put in a 1 litre/1¾ pint jug with 150 ml/½ pint of port or sherry. Cook uncovered on full power for 3 minutes. Stir well to ensure jelly is dissolved.

3. Make up the jelly to 900 ml/1½ pints with water. Do not add too much water.

4. Wet a 1.75 litre/3 pint pudding basin with cold water. Pour the liquid jelly into wet basin.

5. Add to this the grapes, raisins and nuts. Stir occasionally until set. Refrigerate until needed.

6. Turn out and decorate with a sprig of holly.

Serve with single cream.

Grace Mulligan

A tip

To dissolve a packet of jelly. Cut into cubes. Put them in a 1 litre/1¾ pint measuring jug or bowl with 150 ml/¼ pint cold water. Heat on full power for 1½ minutes, or until dissolved. Stir well. Make up to correct volume with cold water or ice cubes. Jellies can be loosened in the bowl or mould to make them easy to turn out: 15 seconds on full power – but remember not to put a metal mould in the microwave cooker.

Joan Tyers

COCOA COFFEE MOUSSE

Serves 4 to 6

2 eggs
50 to 75 g/2 to 3 oz caster sugar
1 teaspoon vanilla essence
4 level teaspoons cocoa
1 level teaspoon instant coffee
300 ml/½ pint milk
3 tablespoons hot water
15 g/½ oz gelatine (1 sachet)
150 ml/5 fl oz double cream
Flaked almonds

1. Separate eggs. Put whites in a clean grease-free basin.

2. In another bowl, put yolks, caster sugar and vanilla essence. Beat until light and creamy.

3. In a 1 litre/1¼ pint jug mix the cocoa and coffee with a little of the measured milk. Stir in the remaining milk. Cook uncovered on full power for 4 minutes.

4. Stir into egg-yolk mixture and cook for 1 minute.

5. Measure 3 tablespoons of hot water in a small bowl. Sprinkle on gelatine. Stir a little just to mix. Leave for 5 minutes to soften. (This water can be heated in the microwave, 30 seconds is enough.)

6. Stir gelatine into chocolate mixture. Leave in a cool place until just on setting point.

7. Whip cream until just thick. Keep 2 tablespoons aside until later for decoration.

8. Whisk egg-whites until stiff but not dry.

9. Using a metal spoon, carefully fold cream and egg-whites into chocolate mixture. Pour into a fluted mould or a nice serving dish. Put in refrigerator to set, allow at least 30 minutes.

10. If using a mould, dip it into a bowl of hand-hot water and turn mousse out on to a serving plate.

11. Put remaining whipped cream in a piping bag with a star nozzle. Pipe on stars to decorate and arrange flaked almonds to look pretty.

Chill until ready to serve.

Dorothy Sleightholme

COLD FRUIT SOUFFLÉ

Can be made with blackberries, blackcurrants, cranberries, plums, raspberries or strawberries.

Enough for 10 people but it is easy to make a smaller quantity, scaling ingredients down to 1 or 2 eggs

900 g/2 lb fruit, fresh or frozen
Water
About 50 g/2 oz sugar
40 g/1½ oz gelatine (3 sachets)
3 large egg-whites

To decorate: chopped nuts, whipped cream for piping (optional)

This can be served in a 1.75 litre/3 pint glass dish or in a specially prepared 1.2 litre/2 pint straight-sided dish. This measures 15 cm/6 inches across and 7.5 cm/3 inches deep. When the soufflé is served it stands up about 3 cm/$1\frac{1}{4}$ inches above the top of the dish.

To prepare a traditional soufflé dish with a paper collar:

1. Cut from a roll of greaseproof paper a single piece measuring 56 cm/22 inches long and 38 cm/15 inches wide.
2. Now fold this lengthways so that you have three thicknesses, 56 cm/22 inches long and 13 cm/5 inches wide.
3. Wind this strip around the outside of the dish and fix it as tightly as you can. Elastic bands are best to hold it in place. It needs to fit very well, especially at rim edge.

Now for the soufflé:

1. Wash fruit and put it in a large (2.75 litre/$4\frac{1}{2}$ to 5 pint) bowl with 5 tablespoons water. Cover and cook on full power for 10 minutes or until soft. Stir halfway through cooking.
2. Put cooked fruit through a nylon sieve, scraping purée from underneath as you do it.
3. Measure purée and, if necessary, top up with water to 1.25 litres/$2\frac{1}{4}$ pints. Return purée to bowl.
4. Add sugar according to taste and stir into purée. Cook uncovered for 4 minutes. Stir well to dissolve the sugar.
5. Heat 3 tablespoons water in a cup, uncovered, on full power for one minute or until just bubbling. Sprinkle on the gelatine and stir until dissolved.
6. Strain gelatine mixture into fruit purée, stir well and leave to set in a cool place, or the refrigerator.
7. When fruit is set but still wobbly take a fork and mix it all up again.
8. In a clean, grease-free bowl, whisk egg-whites until stiff. Fold them into fruit.

9. Pour into prepared dish. If you have used a soufflé dish with paper collar, the soufflé will be about 3 cm/$1\frac{3}{4}$ inches above top of dish. Put it carefully in refrigerator to set. allowing 2 or 3 hours.
10. To serve, peel paper gently away, using the blunt edge of a knife.

Decorate risen edge by gently pressing on chopped nuts. Top can be decorated with a border of chopped nuts or piped rosettes of whipped cream. Otherwise a jug of pouring cream is nice to serve with it.

Grace Mulligan

TO STEW APPLES – AND OTHER FRUITS

600 g/$1\frac{1}{4}$ lb cooking apples, peeled cored and thinly sliced
Caster sugar to taste
3 tablespoons water

Put the fruit, sugar and water in a large (2.75 litre/$4\frac{1}{2}$ to 5 pint) bowl. Cook covered on full power for about 9 minutes, or until the apples are tender. Stir halfway through cooking.

Notes

1. Replace apples, if desired, with pears.
2. The fruit tends to retain its shape. Should a mushy result be desired, it will be necessary to break up with a fork or liquidise after cooking.
3. Soft fruits such as raspberries do not require extra water. Allow a cooking time of about 6 minutes for 450g/1 lb.

To Thaw

Place in a covered bowl. Use full power to thaw partially, then leave to stand. 450 g/1 lb takes about 5 to 6 minutes and should be left to stand for about 10 to 15 minutes.

Marie Emmerson

A tip

To peel peaches. Slit skin or pierce with a fork. Heat on full power: 30 seconds for 1 peach, 1 minute for 2. Skin will peel easily.

Joan Tyers

FUDGE TART

First published in a book of family recipes 'In a Bisley Kitchen', collected over 100 years. This recipe is very easy in the microwave.

For this you need a ready-baked shallow 15 cm/6 inch pastry case.

Serves 4 or more – it is very rich

Filling

50 g/2 oz butter
50 g/2 oz light soft brown sugar
A 196 g/6.91 oz can sweetened condensed milk
25 g/1 oz roughly-chopped walnuts
25 g/1 oz seedless raisins
25 g/1 oz glacé cherries, chopped

1. Put the butter in a 1 litre/1¾ pint jug. Cook on full power, uncovered, for 1 minute.
2. Stir in sugar and condensed milk.
3. Continue cooking for 2 minutes. Stir well to dissolve sugar. Cook for a further 3 to 4 minutes once boiling. Stir every minute. Watch carefully to see that the fudge does not turn too dark or the taste may be spoilt. It should be golden brown.
4. Stir in walnuts, raisins and cherries.
5. Pour mixture into pastry case and leave to cool.

Mrs A Bucknell
Bisley, Gloucestershire

DEVONSHIRE JUNKET

This can be made from pasteurized or farm-bottled milk, but homogenised, sterilised and UHT milk are not suitable. Delicious made with Channel Islands milk.

Serves 4

600 ml/1 pint milk
1 tablespoon sugar
2 teaspoons brandy or rum
1 teaspoon essence of rennet
Cinnamon
Grated nutmeg

1. Put the milk and sugar in a 1 litre/1¾ pint jug. Cook uncovered on full power for 2 to 3 minutes until only blood heat, 98°F, 30°C. Stir to dissolve sugar.
2. Stir in brandy or rum and pour into a nice dish. Without delay, stir in rennet and put dish aside to set at room temperature. It takes about 1½ to 2 hours.
3. When junket is set, sprinkle cinnamon and nutmeg on top. It can then be chilled.

Serve with sugar to taste and Devonshire cream if you can.

Mrs Elizabeth Selby
Exeter

GOOSEBERRY FOOL

Serves 4

450 g/1 lb gooseberries
2 tablespoons sugar, or more to taste
150 ml/¼ pint whipping or double cream

To decorate

Toasted flaked almonds (*see page 107*) **or desiccated coconut** (*see page 109*)

No need to top or tail the berries. Rinse in cold water and drain. Frozen gooseberries can be used.

1. Put the gooseberries in a 2 litre/3½ pint bowl. Cover and cook on full

power for 9 minutes. Stir halfway through cooking. If using gooseberries straight from the freezer, cook 4 minutes longer and stir twice during cooking.
2. Sieve, then sweeten to taste. The purée should not be too thin.
3. Whip cream lightly, preferably using a small balloon whisk – but do not let it get too stiff. Best results are obtained if purée and cream are the same consistency.
4. When purée is cold, carefully fold together with the cream. A few drops of green colouring can be added during folding to enhance the colour, but cooking fruit by microwave produces almost unimpaired colour.

Serve in small glasses. Top with some toasted flaked almonds or coconut.

Mary Watts

ICE-CREAM

Serves 4 to 6

3 eggs
25 g/1 oz caster sugar
300 ml/½ pint milk
Small tin condensed milk

1. Separate whites from yolks of eggs.
2. Whisk yolks and sugar together until lighter in colour.
3. Put the fresh milk into a 600 ml/ 1 pint jug. Cook uncovered on full power for 4 minutes. Pour a little at a time on to the egg yolks, whisking all the time.
4. Pour the mixture into a 1 litre/1¾ pint jug. Cook uncovered on full power for 3 to 4 minutes, or until the mixture coats the back of a wooden spoon. It is important to whisk the mixture every 30 seconds during cooking or it may 'scramble' – but it tastes all right even if it does!
5. Pour mixture into bowl, add condensed milk and mix well. Leave mixture to cool.
6. Pour into a shallow rectangular polythene container (or the refrigerator ice tray with divisions removed) and place in freezing compartment of refrigerator. Leave it

there until ice forms around the edge of the mixture.
7. Then stir the mixture and put it back in the refrigerator or freezer while the egg-whites are whisked.
8. Whisk the egg-whites until stiff and fold into the ice-cream.
9. Place back in the refrigerator or freezer until the ice-cream sets hard.

Try also these flavourings:

Apricot Ice-Cream

1. Drain juice from a 425 g/15 oz tin of apricot halves. Sieve the fruit or liquidise until a purée.
2. Stir in 2 tablespoons of the apricot juice.
3. After folding egg-whites into the ice-cream, fold in the apricot purée and freeze.

Brown Bread Ice-Cream

After folding the stiffly-whisked egg-whites into the ice-cream, fold in 50 g/2 oz fresh brown bread-crumbs and freeze.
1 teaspoon of rum can also be added with the breadcrumbs.

Chocolate Ice-Cream

1. Break up 125 g/4 oz plain chocolate and put it in a small bowl. Cook uncovered on full power for 3 minutes, or until melted.
2. Add 1 dessertspoon golden syrup, mix well and add with the condensed milk at paragraph 5 of the basic recipe.

Sue Probert
Warwick

A tip

To loosen *ice cream* and make it easy to serve: 15 seconds on full power.

Joan Tyers

LEMON DELIGHT

A recipe from the West Sussex Federation of Women's Institutes' book 'Come Cooking Again'. A delightful sweet, set off by the egg-custard which accompanies it. A perfect recipe for the microwave cooker.

Serves 4

425 ml/¾ pint water
25 g/1 oz cornflour
150 g/5 oz sugar
Grated rind and strained juice
of 2 small lemons
2 egg-whites

Custard

300 ml/½ pint milk
2 egg-yolks
1 tablespoon sugar

1. Put all but 2 tablespoons of the water in a 1 litre/1¾ pint jug. Cook uncovered on full power for 5 minutes, or until boiling.
2. Mix cornflour with remaining water, stir it into boiled water, return to microwave and cook for 1 to 1½ minutes. Stir every 30 seconds.
3. Stir in sugar until dissolved. Allow to cool. Add lemon rind and juice.
4. Whisk egg-whites until really firm. Fold into mixture. Pour into a dish, leave to set in a cool place or refrigerator.
5. Make the custard. Put the milk, egg-yolks and sugar in a 600 ml/1 pint jug. Whisk well.
6. Cook uncovered for 3 to 4 minutes. Check and stir frequently. Cook until it thickens but do not allow to boil. When it is thick enough, the mixture will just coat the back of the spoon.

Mrs Janice Langley
Shoreham-by-Sea, West Sussex

LEMON SOLID

An old family recipe which works perfectly in the microwave cooker.

Serves 4

Rind and juice of 2 lemons
125 to 175 g/4 to 6 oz caster
sugar, according to taste
600 ml/1 pint milk
15 g/½ oz gelatine

1. Finely grate rind from the lemons and squeeze the juice.
2. Put lemon rind into a basin with sugar and half the milk.
3. Pour the remaining milk into a 600 ml/1 pint jug. Cook uncovered on full power for 3 to 4 minutes. Sprinkle the gelatine over the milk and stir briskly until dissolved.
4. Mix heated milk with cold milk mixture, stirring to dissolve sugar.
5. Add lemon juice. Don't be alarmed if milk appears to curdle.
6. Pour into a wet jelly mould and leave to set in a cold larder for about 12 hours, or 5 hours in refrigerator.
7. Turn pudding out of mould. It should have separated with a clear jelly at top and 'curds' at bottom.

Mrs Marion Wightman
Piddletrenthide, Dorset

A tip

Lemon rind can be grated and dried to use later for flavouring cakes, etc. Spread it on a plate, no cover, full power for 30 seconds; but watch throughout to see that it does not burn. *See also page 111,* J for Juice, for a tip about squeezing lemons.

Joan Tyers

MINT PARFAIT

Recipes requiring a syrup are much easier to make in a microwave cooker than in a saucepan on top of a stove. This old recipe has converted very successfully.

Serves 4

150 g/5 oz caster sugar
150 ml/¼ pint water
2 egg whites
A pinch of salt
45 ml/3 tablespoons Crême de
  Menthe
275 ml/½ pint double cream,
  whipped to soft peaks

Topping
Grated chocolate or sugared
mint leaves*

1. Put the sugar and water in a 2
litre/3½ pint bowl. Cook uncovered on
full power for 4 minutes. Stir well to
ensure the sugar is dissolved.
2. Continue cooking on full power
until the syrup reaches a temperature
of 238°F, 110°C. It may take 7 minutes.
When the temperature is reached, stir
in a small teaspoonful of cold water to
stop it getting any hotter.
Alternatively, transfer to a heatproof
jug.
If you have not got a thermometer,
the syrup is boiled until it can be
formed into a very soft ball when
tested in a cup of cold water.
3. Whisk egg-whites with salt until
stiff but not dry. While still whisking,
pour on boiling syrup in a steady
stream and keep on whisking until it
has cooled.
4. Mix in Crême de Menthe, then fold
in cream.
5. Put into a covered plastic box and
freeze.

Serve scoops of the parfait sprinkled
with grated plain chocolate, or a
topping of your choice.

*Sugared mint leaves

Paint fresh mint leaves with lightly
beaten egg-white. Coat well with
caster sugar. Allow to dry in a warm
room.

Anne Wallace
Stewarton, Ayrshire

ORANGE CREAM CHEESE CAKE

Best made the day before it is to be
eaten so that flavour matures.

For this you need a loose-bottomed
20 cm/8 inch flan tin or a ring set on a
baking sheet.

Serves 4 to 6

Flan case
100 g/4 oz digestive biscuits
50 g/2 oz butter

Filling
60 g/2½ oz sugar
75 ml/3 fl oz concentrated
  orange juice, the frozen
  variety gives a good strong
  flavour
275 g/10 oz cream cheese
To decorate: finely-grated
  orange rind

1. **Start with the flan case.** Crush
the biscuits by laying them flat in a
single layer inside a large polythene
bag and pressing with a rolling pin.
2. Put the butter in a 600 ml/1 pint
jug. Cook uncovered on full power for
1½ minutes, or until melted.
3. Add crushed biscuits and turn
them over and over until well
integrated with butter.
4. Press the mixture into the flan tin
or ring and leave to firm up.
5. **Now the filling.** Stir sugar and
orange juice together until dissolved.
6. Mix in cream cheese very
gradually until it is all incorporated.
7. Pour this mixture into the biscuit
case and press down gently. Level and
smooth the top.
8. Refrigerate until set.
9. When needed, sit the flan tin on an
upturned basin. The ring will drop
away, leaving you to slide the
cheesecake on to a flat plate. Or, if
using a flan ring, carefully slide
cheesecake and ring on to a flat plate,
then lift off the ring.

Serve with single cream in a jug.

Grace Mulligan

RASPBERRY MOUSSE

This can be frozen and is delicious to
eat frozen or just chilled.

Serves 4

**A 170 g/6 oz can of evaporated
milk
A 369 g/13 oz can of raspberries,
or equal quantity of frozen
raspberries
1 raspberry jelly
To decorate (optional): 150 ml/¼
pint whipped cream**

1. Put evaporated milk into the
refrigerator for about 1 hour so that
it is thoroughly chilled when needed.
2. Drain liquid from can of
raspberries into a measuring jug and
make up with water to 300 ml/½ pint.
3. Rinse out a 600 ml/1 pint jug or
bowl. Cut the jelly into cubes and put
them in the wet dish. (This prevents
jelly sticking to bowl.)
4. Cook uncovered on full power for
1½ minutes to melt jelly cubes. Stir the
liquid until all the jelly has dissolved.
5. Stir the 300 ml/½ pint raspberry
juice into the melted jelly. If using
frozen raspberries, stir in 300 ml/½
pint water. Leave till cool and just
beginning to set.
6. Whisk evaporated milk until thick.
7. Whisk jelly, adding the milk
gradually. It should double its bulk.
8. Fold in raspberries.
9. Leave to set. It will set almost
immediately with frozen raspberries.
10. Decorate by piping with whipped
cream.

Sybil Norcott
Irlam, Nr Manchester

Toasted Coconut. Spread 50 g/2 oz
desiccated coconut in a shallow dish.
Cook uncovered on full power for 5
minutes. Stir twice during cooking
for an even result.

Joan Tyers

SEMOLINA HALVA

Serves 4

**300 g/11 oz coarse semolina
125 g/4 oz butter cut in pieces
600 ml/1 pint milk
275 g/10 oz sugar
50 g/2 oz blanched almonds,
coarsely chopped
A few drops of almond essence
¼ teaspoon saffron powder,
dissolved in ¼ teaspoon water**

1. Using a heavy-based pan, dry-roast
semolina over low heat on top of the
stove until pale brown, stirring
frequently or it will burn.
2. Put the hot semolina into a
medium-sized (2 litre/3½ pint) bowl.
Stir in the butter, milk and sugar.
Cook uncovered on full power for 7
minutes, or until thick. Stir
frequently to avoid lumps.
3. When quite stiff, add almonds,
essence and saffron.
4. Mix thoroughly and pat on to a
buttered tray to about 7 mm/¼ inch
thick.
5. Cut into 2.5 cm/1 inch squares.

Keep in a cool place and eat within a
day or two of making.

Priya Wickramasinghe
Cardiff

SHERRY CHIFFON PIE

For this you need a 20 cm/8 inch case
of short or sweet shortcrust pastry,
baked blind.

Makes one 20 cm/8 inch round pie

Filling

**2 tablespoons sherry
1 dessertspoon gelatine
225 ml/8 fl oz milk
1 large egg, separated
75 g/3 oz caster sugar
¼ teaspoon almond essence
Nutmeg**

1. Measure 1 tablespoon sherry into a
cup, sprinkle on gelatine, and stir
once to combine. Leave to soften.

2. Put the milk in a 600 ml/1 pint jug. Cook uncovered on full power for 2 minutes or until hot.

3. Beat egg-yolk and 50 g/2 oz of the caster sugar in a 1 litre/1¾ pint jug. Stir in the hot milk. Strain into the milk jug, then back.

4. Cook uncovered for 3 to 4 minutes. Stir every minute. Cook until mixture clings to spoon – do not boil.

5. Stir in the gelatine mixture and almond essence. Beat to dissolve gelatine. Add the remaining tablespoon of sherry. Cool until thickening.

6. Whisk egg-white stiffly, then whisk in remaining 25 g/1 oz caster sugar. Fold into the mixture.

7. Pour into cold baked flan case, grate a little nutmeg on top. Leave to set in a cool place.

If there is any risk of the flan case breaking, put it back in its ring on the plate from which it will be served, then pour the mixture in. Remove ring when serving.

Dorothy Sleightholme

Chapter 8

Cakes, Buns, Cookies and Biscuits

Some extra useful information, but not necessary for following the recipes.

This chapter is very short because cakes and biscuits are not the microwave cooker's best product. This is because traditional recipes have been developed to cook by heat. We normally expect a brown crisp exterior and a soft interior. Cooking by microwave does not brown, and most cake mixtures do not benefit from being cooked so quickly. Cakes **can** *be made, but generally the recipe needs to have been specially developed. These are acceptable to many, but should be regarded as 'microwave cakes', which lack colour and are of a different texture.*

Generally, the full power setting is used but fruit cakes benefit from being cooked more slowly on the defrost (30%) setting. Containers should **never be floured**, *as the flour will remain as a thin film on the cooked cake and look and taste unpleasant. Greasing, or lining with clingfilm or greaseproof paper, is of benefit. A cover is not required.*

You can generally tell when cakes are cooked by pressing a skewer or cocktail stick into the centre. If it comes out clean, the cake should be done. The top of the cake may still look a little moist but this dries out on standing.

Small cakes or biscuits are best cooked in a circle and should be checked frequently to avoid overcooking.
See also some tips suggested by Joan Tyers, (page 109, C for Cakes).

Thawing

Many commercially frozen cakes carry microwave instructions about thawing, and it is worth following these. However, if thawing a home baked product place it on a piece of paper towel to absorb moisture and to avoid the base going soggy. Generally, the defrost (30%) setting is used and a cover is not required. With cake-type products, only partial thawing should be given and a long standing time allowed to avoid dehydration. For guidance, give 3 to 4 minutes for a sponge-type cake, then let it stand at room temperature until thawing has completed. For small cakes and slices of cakes, about 15 to 30 seconds should be ample.

BATTENBERG CAKE

Cake

125 g/4 oz margarine
125 g/4 oz caster sugar
2 beaten eggs

125 g/4 oz self-raising white flour
A few drops of pink colouring
1 tablespoon raspberry jam

2 tablespoons apricot jam (or
use raspberry jam throughout)

Almond paste

75 g/3 oz ground almonds
25 g/1 oz semolina
75 g/3 oz caster sugar
75 g/3 oz sifted icing sugar
A few drops of almond essence
Beaten egg to bind
To finish: a little caster sugar

1. Grease two 450 g/1 lb loaf-shaped
containers.
2. Cream margarine and sugar, beat
in eggs, fold in flour.
3. Divide mixture exactly into 2
portions and colour one pink.
4. Place a portion of mixture in each
container.
5. Cook uncovered for 4½ minutes on
full power, until firm to the touch
when gently pressed. The cakes
should be removed from microwave
when the tops are still slightly moist,
but should then dry out on standing.
Leave to stand for 3 to 4 minutes
before turning out of containers on to
a wire rack to cool.
6. Trim sides and level tops.
7. Cut each cake exactly in half
lengthways. All the pieces must be the
same size.
8. Using raspberry jam, sandwich the
four portions together, arranging pink
and white squares alternately.
9. **For the paste.** Combine
ingredients, using enough egg to make
a firm paste.
10. Use a piece of waxed paper,
sprinkle well with caster sugar and on
it roll out paste to fit around the sides
of cake.
11. Spread the paste with sieved
apricot or raspberry jam, place cake on
at one end. Carefully wrap paste round
cake, pressing so that it adheres. Press
edges together to seal.
12. Trim ends of cake, flute along two
top edges, make a diamond pattern on
top with back of knife. Dredge lightly
with caster sugar.

Sybil Norcott
Irlam, Nr Manchester

A tip

When experimenting with cakes
which usually require the creaming
method, put all ingredients together.
Mix well, but do not beat hard as too
much air causes mixture to expand
during cooking and possibly overflow
the container. The cake may then
collapse when taken from microwave
cooker.
The right consistency for a microwave
cake or pudding mixture: it should
drop off the spoon to the count of 3. If
necessary, add 2 or 3 tablespoons cold
water. Too much liquid produces a
heavy result.

Joan Tyers

CHOCOLATE SPONGE SANDWICH

In our tests we found this type of cake
baked by microwave was beautifully
light, like a fatless sponge. However, it
tends to dry out soon after it is made,
and is best eaten within a day or two.
It makes a delicious quick pudding if
eaten hot with chocolate or fudge
sauce (*see page 73*).

Mixed all in one bowl.

To bake this you need a round
container 18 cm/7 inches in diameter
and 9 cm/3½ inches deep.

175 g/6 oz self-raising white flour
175 g/6 oz caster sugar
175 g/6 oz margarine, softened
1 level tablespoon cocoa
1½ level teaspoons baking
powder
3 eggs, use medium or small
eggs
2 tablespoons warm water

1. Grease the container and line it
with greased, greaseproof paper.

2. Put all the ingredients together in a warm bowl, sifting in the cocoa and baking powder. Mix well until smooth. Beating is not required.
3. Spoon the mixture into the container. Make a shallow well in the centre.
4. Cook uncovered on full power for 8½ minutes. Turn the container after 3 and 6 minutes.
5. Leave to stand for 5 minutes before turning out on to a wire rack to cool.

When taken from the microwave, the surface of the cake may be a little sticky, but should otherwise be firm to the touch when gently pressed. The sticky surface should dry out during standing time. If the cake is left to cook longer until stickiness has gone, it will be hard and unpleasant to eat.

Sandwich filling

50 g/2 oz soft margarine
125 to 175 g/4 to 6 oz icing sugar
1 large teaspoon cocoa
1 teaspoon hot water
1 teaspoon sherry or liqueur (optional)

1. Beat margarine in a bowl.
2. Sieve in 125 g/4 oz of the icing sugar and the cocoa.
3. Add other ingredients, including 1 extra teaspoon hot water if sherry is not used.
4. Beat until smooth, sieving in extra icing sugar if necessary.
5. Cut sponge in half and fill with about half of this quantity.
6. Use the rest to spread on top, saving a little to pipe decorations around edge. Nuts or flaked chocolate can also be used to decorate.

Grace Mulligan

To toast flaked almonds: spread 50 g/2 oz flaked almonds on a heatproof plate. Cook uncovered on full power for 6 minutes. Stir them about after 4 minutes, picking out the ones that are already brown enough. When they are quite cold, store in an airtight jar.

Joan Tyers

Another tip: This mixture can be baked as small buns. The whole quantity is enough for 27. Use two paper bun-cases together, which will make a stronger container than one and keep the buns in a better shape as they cook. Cook in batches, 10 at a time, arranged in a ring around turntable, or on a large plate. Cook on full power, 2 minutes for 10 buns, 1½ minutes for 7.

Joan Tyers

VICTORIA SPONGE

Grace Mulligan was not really pleased with the results of her test with this classic recipe. It is included because you may like to try your own skill at microwave baking, and if you succeed please let us know! Using half wholewheat and half white flour and light, soft brown sugar instead of caster, improves the look of the cake. At least it can be served hot as a pudding if all else fails.

125 g/4 oz margarine
125 g/4 oz caster sugar
2 large eggs
125 g/4 oz self-raising white flour

To Finish

2 tablespoons raspberry jam
2 teaspoons caster sugar

1. Grease one deep, round container, 17 to 18 cm/6½ to 7 inches in diameter, and line the base with greased, greaseproof paper.
2. Beat margarine and sugar until creamy.
3. Add eggs one at a time, beating and adding 2 teaspoonfuls of the flour to prevent curdling.
4. Fold in rest of flour. Pour into container.
5. Cook uncovered on full power for 5 minutes. The top will be slightly tacky but should dry out on standing. Let it stand for 5 minutes before turning out on to a wire rack to cool.
6. When cold, peel off paper, split cake in half, then sandwich together with raspberry jam.
7. Sprinkle caster sugar lightly on top.

A tip

Custard powder can be used to improve the colour of cakes or puddings made with white flour. Substitute 15 g/½ oz custard powder for 15 g/½ oz of the flour.

Joan Tyers

MRS ROBIN'S FRUIT CAKE

It is hard to make a mistake with this reliable old recipe, even in a microwave cooker, although the result is not quite so brown and shiny as when baked in an ordinary oven. It produces a good, everyday cake and is even suitable as a simple Christmas cake, especially if iced with sherry butter icing. It is important to use dark sugar and 125 g/4 oz of the flour should be wholewheat, either the plain or the self-raising. Be sure to use the correct size and shape of microwave baking container; the heavy plastic type is ideal.

125 g/4 oz margarine
175 g/6 oz dark soft brown sugar
175 g/6 oz currants
175 g/6 oz sultanas
50 g/2 oz candied peel
225 ml/8 fl oz water
1 level teaspoon bicarbonate of soda
1 heaped teaspoon of mixed spice
2 beaten eggs
125 g/4 oz plain wholewheat flour
125 g/4 oz self raising flour
Pinch of salt

1. Put margarine cut in pieces, sugar, currants, sultanas, peel, water, bicarbonate of soda and mixed spice into a medium-sized (2 litre/3½ pint) bowl. Cook uncovered on full power for 4 minutes. Stir after 3 minutes. Set aside to cool.
2. Grease a 20 cm/8 inch round baking container and line the bottom with greased, greaseproof paper.
3. Add eggs, flours and salt to cooled mixture, mix well, pour into baking container.
4. Stand the container on a rack and cook uncovered on defrost (30%) setting for 40 minutes. The surface of the cake should then be nicely dry all over, and you can test if it is done by spearing the centre with a skewer. If it comes out clean, the cake is done.
5. Let it stand 15 minutes before turning out on to a wire rack.

Mary Watts/Joan Tyers

A tip

Jam for pouring over sponge puddings, etc. Remove metal lid, put jar of jam into microwave cooker on full power for 1 minute. Jam sets again when cold.

Joan Tyers

Royal Icing. If you have variable power settings, lattice work and fine piped designs, which require drying and usually take days, can be dried in the microwave cooker on low or warm (10%) setting, giving 15 second bursts with 3 minute rests in between.

Joan Tyers

FLAPJACKS

These cook almost as well in a microwave as in an ordinary oven, but are a bit 'chewy'.

Makes 15

75 g/3 oz margarine
2 tablespoons golden syrup or
  black treacle
75 g/3 oz Barbados sugar
150 g/5 oz porridge oats

1. Lightly grease a 20 cm/8 inch shallow container.
2. Put the margarine and syrup or treacle into a 1 litre/1¾ pint jug. Cook uncovered on full power for 3 minutes, or until margarine has melted.
3. Stir in sugar and rolled oats. Mix well.
4. Spread mixture evenly into container.
5. Cook uncovered on full power for 3½ to 4 minutes. Turn around halfway through cooking and level mixture again, but take care as it is very hot.
6. Leave to cool in container for 5 minutes. Mark into fan shaped pieces and allow to go cold in the container.
7. When cold, break into pieces.

Flapjacks improve with keeping. Store in an airtight tin for up to 4 weeks.

Try these variations:

1. Add 2 rounded teaspoons grated orange rind and 50 g/2 oz currants to mixture at stage 3 of recipe.
2. Replace 25 g/1 oz of the rolled oats with 25 g/1 oz desiccated coconut.

Dorothy Sleightholme

Meringues. It is possible to cook them if the microwave cooker has variable power settings, including warm or 10%. A batch of a dozen can be made from 2 egg-whites and 100 g/4 oz sugar. Pipe in small rosettes on to vegetable parchment (Bakewell paper) on the microwave turntable. Cooking is done on warm or low (10%) setting in 15 second bursts, followed by 15 second rests. Repeat 2 or 3 times until meringues are dry. Store in airtight tin. Do not try to hurry the cooking or the sugar will carbonize inside the meringue.

Joan Tyers

LEMON CUSTARD CAKE

The cake cannot be baked successfully in a microwave cooker, but the custard filling works well.

For the cake you need a 20 cm/8 inch cake tin with a removable base.

Custard filling

25 g/1 oz cornflour
300 ml/½ pint milk
2 egg-yolks
2 dessertspoons sugar
Rind and juice of ½ lemon
3 dessertspoons lemon curd (*see page 100*)

Cake

225 g/8 oz self-raising flour
125 g/4 oz margarine
75 g/3 oz sugar
1 beaten egg
¼ teaspoon vanilla or almond
  essence
A little milk
A little egg-white

Make the filling first:

1. Mix cornflour in a 600 ml/l pint jug with a little of the milk. Stir in the sugar and gradually mix in the rest of the milk.
2. Cook uncovered on full power for 4 minutes. Whisk every minute to avoid lumps.
3. Beat in the egg-yolks. They should cook from the heat of the sauce.
4. Beat in the lemon rind, juice and lemon curd. Leave this custard to cool.

For the cake:

5. Put flour in a bowl and rub in margarine.
6. Mix in sugar, beaten egg, vanilla or almond essence. Add a little milk, a tablespoon at a time, and mix to a stiff, scone-like consistency.
7. Grease the cake tin and line base with greased, greaseproof paper.
8. Roll out just over half the mixture to a round about 27 cm/10½ inches across.
9. Fit this into the tin and fill with cooled custard mixture.
10. Brush top edges of cake base with a little egg-white.
11. Roll out remaining cake mixture and fit on top, pressing lightly round edges to seal it in place. Brush top with egg-white.
12. Bake in centre of a moderate oven, Gas 4, 350°F, 180°C, for about 30 minutes until quite firm and golden on top.
13. Lift out of tin on removable base and slide off base on to a cooling wire.

Serve warm or cooled as a sweet course or at tea-time. When cool, serve with a little cream.

Mrs Carol Goldsmith
Beccles, Suffolk

A tip

Lemon rind can be grated and dried to use later for flavouring cakes, etc. Spread it on a plate, no cover, full power for 30 seconds; but watch throughout to see that it does not burn. *See also page 111*, J for Juice, for a tip about squeezing lemons.

Joan Tyers

BUTTER CREAM MOUSSE

This is much less sweet than ordinary butter cream and is excellent for filling cakes.

The quantity given here would fill two cakes

50 g/2 oz caster sugar
65 ml/2½ fl oz water
2 egg-yolks
100 g/4 oz unsalted or slightly
  salted butter
Coffee essence or rum to flavour

1. Put the sugar and water in a 600 ml/1 pint jug. Cook uncovered on full power for 2 minutes. Stir well to dissolve the sugar. Continue cooking till the syrup is sticky and will pull a thread between finger and thumb. Cool slightly.
2. Beat egg-yolks, pour syrup over them and whisk until thick.
3. Cream the butter and gradually beat mousse mixture into it.
4. Flavour with coffee essence or rum.

Keeps for a week in a covered container in refrigerator.

Mrs Joan Hudson
Finsthwaite, Ulverston, Cumbria

CHOCOLATE BUTTER CREAM

125 g/4 oz plain cooking chocolate
125 g/4 oz butter or table margarine
175 g/6 oz icing sugar

1. Break up chocolate and place in a 600 ml/1 pint jug. Cook uncovered on full power for 2 minutes or until melted. Stir well. Avoid overcooking or flavour and texture may be spoilt.
2. Cream butter or margarine and icing sugar until smooth and cream in colour. (If butter is taken straight out of refrigerator put it in a bowl in the microwave cooker on full power for 15 seconds to soften – but do not let it melt.) Add melted chocolate and beat again.

This filling is worth making in this quantity as it keeps in a cool place or refrigerator for quite some time and can be used as required to fill or top cakes or biscuits. If too firm to spread, beat up with a very little boiling water when using.

Nice also if you add 2 or 3 teaspoons sherry or brandy with the chocolate.

Anne Wallace
Stewarton, Ayrshire

Fondant icing can be softened on defrost (30%) setting, allowing 2 to 3 minutes per 450 g/1 lb. Leave it in wrapper or covered with clingfilm.

Joan Tyers

SOFT GINGERBREAD

As it is very difficult to bake really good cakes in a microwave cooker, here it can be used as an aid, then the cake is baked in the conventional oven.

This cake will bake in a 23 cm/9 inch square tin, a 19 by 29 cm/7½ to 11½ inch dripping tin, or in a 900 g/2 lb loaf tin.

125 g/4 oz butter
125 g/4 oz golden syrup
150 g/5 oz dark treacle
125 g/4 oz granulated sugar
275 g/10 oz plain flour
½ teaspoon salt
2 teaspoons ground ginger
1 teaspoon cinnamon
1 level teaspoon bicarbonate of soda
1 beaten egg
225 ml/7 to 8 fl oz sour milk, or half milk and half natural yoghurt

To measure syrup and treacle accurately, first stand the tin in a bowl or a pan of hot water for 5 minutes. Then put empty mixing bowl on scales and pour in the exact quantity.

1. Grease tin and line with greased, greaseproof paper.
2. Put butter, syrup, treacle and sugar in a 2 litre/3½ pint bowl. Cook uncovered on full power for 3 minutes. Stir after 2 minutes to dissolve sugar and again after the 3 minutes. Allow to cool.
3. Sieve together flour, salt, ginger, cinnamon and bicarbonate of soda.
4. Pour treacle mixture into flour.
5. Beat in egg and milk.
6. Pour into prepared tin.
7. Bake in a moderate oven, Gas 3, 325°F, 170°C for about 1 hour. Could take 15 minutes longer in the loaf tins.
8. Turn out of tin on to wire rack to cool.

Dorothy Sleightholme

YORKSHIRE PARKIN

Cakes like this do not bake well in a microwave, but it is useful for melting the fat and syrup.

250 g/9 oz plain wholewheat or white flour
200 g/7 oz brown or white sugar

90 g/3½ oz porridge oats
2 heaped teaspoons powdered
  ginger
75 g/3 oz soft margarine
50 g/2 oz lard
200 g/7 oz golden syrup
75 g/3 oz black treacle*
1 slightly rounded teaspoon
  bicarbonate of soda
A few drops (about 1
  dessertspoon) vinegar
150 ml/¼ pint milk

*If you have no treacle use 275 g/10
oz golden syrup. Add 1 or 2 drops of
gravy browning when you stir the
mixture at paragraph 5, to get the
dark parkin colour.*

1. Mix the flour, sugar, oats and
ginger together in a bowl and make a
well in centre.
2. Put the margarine and lard in a 1
litre/1¾ pint jug. Cook on full power
uncovered for 2 minutes, or until
melted. Add the syrup and cook for a
further 30 seconds to one minute to
warm. Do not overheat, certainly do
not boil.
3. Pour this mixture into dry
ingredients in bowl. Drop bicarbonate
of soda into centre, sprinkle the
vinegar on the soda and watch it fizz.
4. Pour the milk into the syrup jug,
cook uncovered for 30 seconds on full
power, just to warm it. Swirl it around
the jug to clean up the syrup, then add
to the bowl.
5. Now stir it all up well. When
mixed, it should pour like a batter
mixture. Pour it into a large greased
and floured roasting tin.
6. Bake slightly above the middle of a
moderate oven, between Gas 3 and 4,
335°F, 175°C, for 1 hour. Look at it
after 15 to 20 minutes to see if middle
has lifted. If so, shake it to let it sink
again, turn tin round and allow to
continue cooking.
7. Allow to cool in tin. Cut into
quarters. Best if stored 3 days before
eating. Keeps well if stored in an
airtight container.

Mrs Nan Moran
Addingham, Yorkshire

A tip

Breadbaking is not a great success in
a microwave cooker. However, it is
handy for warming flour. The packet
may be put into the microwave cooker
on full power: 1.3 kg/3 lb for 1 minute.

Grace Mulligan

DATE BARS

Makes 6 to 8

225 g/8 oz sweet biscuits
125 g/4 oz margarine
50 to 125 g/2 to 4 oz sugar
225 g/8 oz chopped dates

1. Break up and crush the biscuits,
but not too fine.
2. Put the margarine and sugar in a 1
litre/1¾ pint jug. Cook uncovered on
full power for 3½ minutes. Stir well to
dissolve sugar.
3. Add chopped dates, mix well and
cook uncovered for 1 or 2 minutes.
4. Remove and add crushed biscuits.
Mix well.
5. Press into a shallow, greased Swiss
roll tin. Leave to cool.
6. Cut into bars when cold.

May be iced with melted chocolate
before cutting into bars. Or dip the
ends into melted chocolate. Chocolate
is easily melted in a microwave
cooker: 125 g/4 oz, break into pieces
and put into a small bowl or jug. Cook
uncovered on full power for 3 minutes,
or until melted. Stir well. Avoid
overheating or flavour and texture
may be spoilt.

Sybil Norcott
Irlam, Nr Manchester

SHORTBREAD TOFFEE
PIECES

Successful shortbread must be baked
in an ordinary oven. Results in a

microwave are not as good. However, the microwave is excellent for the soft toffee layer and the chocolate topping.

Makes about 16

Shortbread

125 g/4 oz margarine
50 g/2 oz caster sugar
150 g/5 oz self-raising white or
  brown flour

Toffee

125 g/4 oz margarine
125 g/4 oz caster sugar
2 tablespoons golden syrup
Approximately 200 g/7 oz
  condensed milk: either one
  small can or half a larger one

Topping

125 g/4 oz plain cooking
  chocolate

1. **Shortbread base.** Cream margarine and sugar. Mix in flour. Spread in a greased 28 by 18 cm/11 by 7 inch Swiss roll tin.
2. Bake above centre of a moderate oven, Gas 4, 350°F, 180°C, for 20 minutes. Allow to cool in tin.
3. **Toffee.** Put the margarine, sugar, syrup and milk in a 2 litre/3½ pint jug. Cook uncovered on full power for 5 minutes, or until the mixture leaves the sides of the jug. Stir frequently during cooking and take care because it boils up high in the jug.
4. Pour over the cooled shortbread and leave to cool.
5. **Topping.** Break chocolate into a 600 ml/1 pint jug. Cook uncovered on full power for 3 minutes, or until melted. Stir well. Spread melted chocolate over toffee. Allow to cool.
6. Turn out on to a board and cut into small pieces.

Grace Mulligan

SHERRY SLICES

225 g/8 oz marzipan

Filling

¾ cup digestive biscuit crumbs
½ cup desiccated coconut
½ cup mixed dried fruit, chopped
¼ cup chopped nuts
½ cup raspberry jam
1 tablespoon icing sugar
1 dessertspoon cocoa
1 to 2 tablespoons sherry
To finish: about 175 g/6 oz plain
  cooking chocolate.

1. You need a tin about 23 cm/9 inches square.
2. Divide marzipan in half. Using a board dusted with icing sugar or cornflour, roll each piece out to measure 23 cm/9 inches square. Put one piece in tin.
3. Mix all the filling ingredients, spread over marzipan and put on the marzipan top.
4. Break chocolate into a 600 ml/1 pint jug. Cook uncovered on full power for 4 minutes or until melted. Check and stir frequently to avoid overheating.
5. Spread melted chocolate over and leave till cold.
6. Slice into small fingers.

Judith Adshead
Porth Colmon, Pwllheli, Gwynedd

A tip

To *heat the teapot* while kettle is boiling. Run in 3 or 4 tablespoons cold water from the tap, put on the lid. Heat on full power for 2 minutes. Remember not to put a metal or metal-trimmed pot into the microwave cooker.

Mary Watts

Chapter 9

Preserves and Home-made Sweets

Jams, chutneys and confectionery cook well in a microwave cooker, but it is only suitable for **fairly small quantities.** *If you require large quantities, then the conventional method is the answer. Bottling in a microwave is not advised as, to date, there is insufficient evidence that the process is successful. While jars can be warmed in the microwave cooker (see a tip of Joan Tyers' on page 112, P for Preserves), if you want to sterilize jars this should be carried out in the conventional manner.*

Unless instructions are given to the contrary, a cover should not be used, and the container must be **large enough to prevent boiling over.** *As preserves and confectionery have such a high sugar content, it is essential to use a container which can withstand the high boiling temperature of sugar, and it should always be handled with an oven cloth as it gets very hot.*

Cooking jams, chutneys and confectionery in a microwave is virtually the same as cooking on a hob, but sometimes chutney recipes contain less liquid. Initially, it is wise to follow a microwave recipe until you have gained experience, then you can try your own recipes.

RAW RASPBERRY JAM

A very old Scottish recipe. Tastes delicious and has a lovely bright-red colour.

Yields 900 g/2 lb

450 g/1 lb raspberries
450 g/1 lb caster sugar

1. Crush fruit slightly.
2. Put sugar to warm in a very cool oven, Gas ¼, 225°F, 110°C. Put clean jars to warm in oven also.
3. Put fruit in a large (2.75 litre/4½ to 5 pint) bowl. Cook covered for 6 minutes on full power. Stir halfway through cooking.
4. Stir in warm sugar. Cook for 5 minutes, or until jam reaches boiling point. Stir well halfway through cooking to ensure sugar is dissolved.
5. Allow to stand for about 10 minutes before putting into jars.

> Mrs W White and Mrs S Marshall
> St Michaels, Kent

PLUM BUTTER

Any plums, including greengages or damsons, may be used.

Yields 350 g/¾ lb

450 g/1 lb plums
Approximately 150 ml/5 fl oz honey
¼ teaspoon ground allspice, to taste
¼ teaspoon ground nutmeg, to taste

1. Put plums into a large (2.75 litre/4½ to 5 pint) bowl. Cover and cook on full power for 7 minutes, or until tender.
2. Put plums through a sieve to make a purée.
3. Measure purée in a measuring jug and put back in bowl.
4. Now measure out honey to exactly half the quantity of purée. Add this to the bowl with just enough of the spices to flavour it gently.
5. Cook slowly, uncovered, on full power, stirring often, until it is thick and creamy with no loose liquid. It will take about 13 minutes.
6. Meanwhile, prepare clean jars with airtight lids and put jars to dry and warm in a very cool oven, Gas ¼, 225°F, 110°C.
7. Pour hot, plum butter into warmed jars. Put on airtight lids at once. Label with name and date.

This will not keep for more than a few weeks.

Grace Mulligan

GOOSEBERRY CURD

Delicious as a filling for tartlets and sponges. Also in meringue baskets, but fill them, of course, at the very last minute. Keeps for 6 weeks. Best kept in a refrigerator.

Yields 1 kg/2 to 2½ lbs

675 g/1½ lb young green gooseberries*
300 ml/½ pint water (if gooseberries are ripe use 200 ml/just over ¼ pint)
125 g/4 oz butter, cut in small pieces
325 g/12 oz sugar
3 large eggs, lightly beaten

If you cannot get young gooseberries, 1 or 2 drops of green food colouring can be used to achieve the same bright colour given by green fruit.

1. There is no need to top and tail gooseberries. Put them with the water into a 2.75 litre/4½ to 5 pint bowl. Cover. Cook on full power for 6

minutes. Stir. Continue cooking uncovered for a further 6 minutes.
2. Push gooseberries through a nylon sieve, taking care to scrape purée from underside of sieve.
3. Meanwhile, put sugar in a bowl and cook uncovered on full power for 3 or 4 minutes until warm. Stir frequently.
4. Stir the sugar into the purée. Cook uncovered for 3 minutes. Stir to dissolve sugar.
5. Whisk in the butter and eggs. Cook uncovered for 3 to 4 minutes, or until mixture thickens. Whisk every minute.
6. Pour into warmed jars. Put a waxed tissue on top.
7. When quite cold, put on jam pot covers.

Grace Mulligan

LEMON CURD

The microwave cooker is ideal for lemon curd, saving time dramatically compared with the traditional method. The flavour is good, but the texture is perhaps a little less silky.

Yields 450 g/1 lb

125 g/4 oz butter
175 to 225 g/6 to 8 oz caster sugar*
2 large lemons, rind and juice
2 large eggs, beaten

Use 175 g/6 oz sugar for a sharp taste, 225 g/8 oz sugar for a sweeter curd.

1. Put butter, sugar, lemon rind and half of the strained lemon juice into a 2.75 litre/4½ to 5 pint bowl. Cook uncovered on full power for 3 minutes. Stir halfway through cooking.
2. Stir well until butter has melted and sugar has dissolved.
3. Add remainder of strained lemon juice and beaten eggs.
4. Continue cooking uncovered for 5 minutes, or until mixture has thickened enough to coat the back of a spoon. Check and stir every minute.

Note: the curd tends to thicken more as it cools in the jars. If for some reason it does not, return mixture to jug and beat in another egg-yolk. Continue to cook on full power, stirring every minute as before.
5. Pour into small, hot jam jars – glass baby-food jars are ideal. Cover surface immediately with waxed paper disc. Cover with a clean cloth until quite cold, then fasten on jam pot covers.

Store in refrigerator if possible, and use within 6 weeks.

See page 94, Lemon Custard Cake, for a delicious way to use Lemon curd.

Grace Mulligan

Juice of oranges and lemons will be easier to extract if the whole fruit is warmed for 15 seconds on full power before squeezing.

Joan Tyers

CRANBERRY & ORANGE PRESERVE

Delicious with roast turkey. Sets like jelly.

450 g/1 lb fresh or frozen cranberries
Finely-grated rind and juice of 1 orange
Water
450 g/1 lb granulated sugar

Yields about 900 g/2 lb

1. Put clean 225 g/½ lb jars to warm in the ordinary oven on lowest heat, Gas ¼, 225°F, 110°C.
2. Pick over fruit and discard any that is bruised. Put cranberries into a roomy bowl.

3. Mix orange juice with water to make 300 ml/½ pint. Add to bowl with rind.
4. Cook uncovered for 6 minutes. Reduce to defrost (30%) setting. Cook covered for 10 minutes.
5. Push pulp through a nylon sieve to make a purée, scraping as much as possible from under the sieve.
6. Put sugar in a large (2.75 litre/4½ to 5 pint) bowl. Cook uncovered on full power for 3 minutes or until warm. Stir frequently.
7. Mix purée with sugar and stir until sugar is dissolved.
8. Cook uncovered on full power for 6 to 10 minutes, until the preserve has boiled for 4 to 5 minutes.
9. Pour hot preserve into prepared jars.

Grace Mulligan

KENTISH APPLE CHUTNEY

Traditionally made late in winter with stored apples. A mild, sweet, firm chutney, quick to make.

Yields about 900 g/2 lb

450 g/1 lb apples
300 ml/½ pint spiced pickling vinegar
225 g/½ lb sugar
¾ teaspoon salt
½ teaspoon ground allspice
50 g/2 oz preserved ginger
150 g/6 oz sultanas

1. Peel, core and chop apples into small pieces.
2. Put vinegar, sugar, salt and allspice into a large (2.75 litre/4½ to 5 pint) bowl. Cook covered on full power for 6 minutes. Stir well to dissolve sugar. Set aside.
3. Put apples into a medium-sized (2 litre/3½ pint) bowl. Cook covered for 6 minutes, or until they begin to break down or 'fall'.
4. Stir apples into the vinegar. Wash syrup from ginger, dry and chop into very small pieces. Add to bowl with sultanas.

5. Cook uncovered on full power for 16 minutes or until thick. It will thicken more as it cools.

Chutney is thick enough when a spoon drawn through the mixture leaves its trail and does not at once fill with liquid.

6. Meanwhile, choose jars with vinegar-proof lids. Coffee jars with plastic lids are ideal. Put clean jars to warm in a very cool oven, Gas ¼, 225°F, 110°C.

7. Allow chutney to cool slightly before putting it into jars. Put on waxed paper discs and, when chutney is quite cold, put on vinegar-proof lids.

8. Label with name and date and store in a cool, dry, well-ventilated cupboard.

Allow to mature for 6 weeks before eating.

Mrs Jill Marshall
Kent

DATE CHUTNEY

This chutney is normally made in small quantities, to be eaten straight away.

Keeps well.

Yields about 450 g/1 lb

225 g/8 oz dates
350 ml/12 fl oz malt vinegar
6 tablespoons demerara or
** muscovado sugar**
4 cloves of garlic, finely-
** chopped**
1 teaspoon fresh ginger, finely-
** chopped**
50 g/2 oz sultanas
2 teaspoons paprika
½ to 1 teaspoon salt

1. Chop dates quite small.
2. Put the vinegar and sugar in a large (2.75 litre/4½ to 5 pint) bowl. Cook, covered, on full power for 6 minutes. Stir several times to dissolve the sugar. The mixture should come to the boil.
3. Add dates, garlic, ginger, sultanas, paprika and salt. Cook, uncovered, for

102

8 to 10 minutes until thick. Stir frequently. Do not overcook, or it will turn to caramel.
4. Allow to cool, then pot in clean jars with vinegar-proof lids.

Priya Wickramasinghe
Cardiff

DATE AND BANANA CHUTNEY

Can be made at any time of year. Good with curry. Leave to mature for at least 3 months before eating.

Yields 1.5 kg/3½ lbs

450 g/1 lb onions
225 g/8 oz dates
125 g/4 oz crystallised ginger
2 level teaspoons salt
300 ml/½ pint vinegar
6 bananas
225 g/8 oz black treacle
1 teaspoon curry powder

1. Peel and chop onions finely.
2. Chop up dates and crystallised ginger.
3. Put these into a 2.75 litre/4½ to 5 pint bowl with the salt and half the vinegar. Cover. Cook on full power for 10 minutes. Stir halfway through cooking.
4. Peel and chop up bananas and add them to the bowl with the treacle, curry powder and rest of vinegar.
5. Cook uncovered on full power for 10 minutes. Reduce to defrost (30%) setting. Continue cooking for 15 minutes until all is soft and consistency is thick. When you draw the spoon through it the trail should remain and not at once fill with excess liquid.
6. Meanwhile, choose jars with vinegar-proof lids. Coffee jars with plastic lids are ideal. Paper covers are not satisfactory because vinegar can evaporate through them and chutney will dry out. Plain metal lids should not be used because vinegar corrodes the metal. Put clean jars into a very cool oven to dry and warm, Gas ¼, 225°F, 110°C.

7. Fill warm jars nearly to the brim with hot chutney. Let the chutney go quite cold before putting on the lids.
8. Label and date chutney. Store in a cool, dark place.

Sybil Norcott
Irlam, Nr Manchester

ELDERBERRY CHUTNEY

A sharp chutney.
Let chutney mature for 3 months before eating. It will keep for years if correctly covered and stored.

Yields about 700 g/1½ lb

**1.2 litres/2 pints elderberries
125 g/4 oz seedless raisins
125 g/4 oz demerara sugar
50 g/2 oz onions
15 g/½ oz salt
Pinch cayenne pepper
Pinch allspice
450 ml/¾ pint cider vinegar or
good malt vinegar**

1. Wash elderberries if necessary. Remove them from stalks by running a fork down the stems.
2. Put all the ingredients, except vinegar, in a 2.75 litre/4½ to 5 pint bowl. Cover. Cook on full power for 15 minutes. Stir once or twice during cooking.
3. Stir well to dissolve sugar. Add vinegar.
4. Cook uncovered on full power for 10 minutes. Reduce to defrost (30%) setting. Continue cooking for 20 minutes, or until consistency is thick. Stir once or twice during cooking. When you draw a spoon through it the mark should remain without filling at once with liquid.
5. Meanwhile, choose small jars with vinegar-proof lids. Jars with plastic lids are ideal. Paper covers are not satisfactory because vinegar can evaporate through them and chutney will dry out. Plain metal lids should not be used because vinegar corrodes the metal. Put clean jars into a very cool oven to dry and warm, Gas ¼, 225°F, 110°C.

6. Fill warmed jars nearly to the brim with hot chutney. Put lids on at once.
7. Label and date jars. Store in a cool, dark place.

Mrs Doreen Allars
Meriden, Nr Coventry

PLUM CHUTNEY

Can be made with all types of plums, but dark-skinned varieties give it the best colour.

Yields 1.3 kg/3 lb

**700 g/1½ lb plums
225 g/8 oz onions, finely-chopped
450 g/1 lb cooking apples
300 ml/8 fl oz cider vinegar
A piece of root ginger
1 teaspoon each of whole cloves,
  whole all-spice and
  peppercorns
225 g/8 oz soft brown sugar
1 teaspoon salt**

1. Wipe the plums and cut up roughly.
2. Put onions in a small bowl. Cover. Cook on full power for 3 minutes. Stir once during this time.
3. Peel, core and chop apples. Put them with the plums into a large (2.75 litre/4½ to 5 pint) bowl. Cover. Cook on full power for 6 minutes, or until tender. Stir once or twice during this time.
4. Meanwhile, bruise the ginger by hitting it with a hammer. Then tie it with the other spices in a piece of muslin.
5. Put spice bag with vinegar and sugar into a 1.2 litre/2 pint bowl or jug. Cook uncovered for 6 minutes. Stir to dissolve the sugar. Let it stand for 30 minutes to infuse. Remove spice bag.
6. Pick out the plum stones with a slotted spoon. Add onions, vinegar syrup and salt to bowl. Cook uncovered on full power for 20 minutes, or until chutney is thick. Stir several times during cooking.
7. Pot into clean, warmed jars and put on vinegar-proof lids.

8. Label and store for 4 weeks so that chutney matures and flavour mellows before it is eaten.

Grace Mulligan

PRUNE CHUTNEY

Easy to make half quantity.

Yields 1·3 to 1·8 kg/3 to 4 lb

900 g/2 lb prunes
450 g/1 lb onions, sliced
25 g/1 oz salt
1 teaspoon ground ginger
1 teaspoon cayenne pepper
50 g/2 oz mustard seed
25 g/1 oz mixed pickling spice,
tied up in a little piece of cloth
or nylon curtain
600 ml/1 pint vinegar
450 g/1 lb soft brown sugar

1. Soak prunes for 48 hours in just enough water to cover. This process can be hastened in the microwave cooker (*see page 113*), but they may still have to be left to soak for some time to be soft enough to remove stones easily.
2. Drain off water and remove stones.
3. Put prunes and onions through mincer or food processor into a 2.75 litre/4½ to 5 pint bowl.
4. Add all the other ingredients.
5. Cook uncovered on full power for 20 minutes, or until the mixture is thick. Stir from time to time to ensure even cooking. Chutney is ready if no liquid is visible when a wooden spoon is drawn through the mixture.
6. Pot into clean jars and, when cold, cover with vinegar-proof lids. Label and store in a cool dark place.

Dorothy Sleightholme

TOMATO RELISH

Yields about 1.3 kg/3 lb

1 kg/2 lb firm ripe tomatoes (or
use canned tomatoes)
450 g/1 lb onions, finely-chopped

½ teaspoon salt
450 g/1 lb sugar
50 g/2 oz demerara sugar
15 g/½ oz fresh ginger, finely-
chopped
A pinch of chilli powder
250 ml/7 fl oz malt vinegar

1. Skin the tomatoes. To do this, put them in a basin and pour over boiling water to cover. Leave for 1 minute, then drain and cover with cold water for 2 to 3 minutes. Skins can then be easily removed.
2. Put the onions in a large (2.75 litre/4½ to 5 pint) bowl. Cover. Cook on full power for 8 minutes. Stir after 4 minutes.
3. Chop tomatoes. Add these and all the other ingredients, except the vinegar, to the bowl of onions.
4. Cook uncovered for 8 minutes. Stir. Reduce to defrost (30%) setting. Cook for 20 minutes or until thick. Stir regularly.
5. Add vinegar and cook uncovered on full power for another 6 minutes.
6. Pour the mixture while hot into warmed, clean dry jars with vinegar-proof lids.
7. Put on the lids when relish is cold. Label and store in a cool, dry place.

Priya Wickramasinghe
Cardiff

RICH FUDGE

50 g/2 oz butter
50 g/2 oz light soft brown sugar
A 196 g/6.91 oz can of sweetened
condensed milk
25 g/1 oz roughly-chopped
walnuts
25 g/1 oz seedless raisins
25 g/1 oz glacé cherries, chopped

1. Put the butter in a 1 litre/1¾ pint jug. Cook uncovered on full power for 1 minute.
2. Stir in sugar and condensed milk.
3. Continue cooking for 2 minutes. Stir well to dissolve sugar. Cook for a further 3 to 4 minutes once boiling. Stir every minute. Watch carefully to see that the fudge does not turn too

dark or the taste may be spoilt. It should be golden brown.

4. Stir in walnuts, raisins and cherries.

5. Pour mixture into a well-greased, 18 cm/7 inch square tin. Leave to cool, then cut into small squares.

Mrs A Bucknell
Bisley, Gloucestershire

GLACÉ FRUITS

Fresh fruits such as strawberries, orange or mandarin segments, clusters of two grapes, etc., are dipped in caramel, giving them a shiny crisp coating. Canned fruit can also be used, including maraschino cherries, providing the syrup is dried off carefully before they are dipped in the caramel.

Preparing a syrup in a microwave is a distinct improvement on the saucepan on top of a stove. There is less risk of burning and the syrup remains liquid throughout the dipping, whereas it has a tendency to set in the saucepan before it is all used.

Lovely for a party, but cannot be made too far ahead as they go sticky in a day or so, particularly if weather is humid.

The quantity of syrup given is *enough to coat about 20 pieces of fruit.* You will need tiny, crinkled paper sweet cases which can be bought at good stationers. Also, several wooden cocktail sticks for dipping. It is useful, but not essential, to have a sugar thermometer.

Syrup for caramel

100 g/4 oz sugar
60 ml/2½ fl oz hot water
5 ml/1 teaspoon glucose

1. Brush baking trays lightly with oil.
2. Prepare fruit, making sure it is clean and thoroughly dried.

3. Put the sugar and hot water in a 1 litre/1¾ pint jug. Cook uncovered on full power for 2 minutes. Stir well to dissolve the sugar.
4. Add glucose. Cook on full power for 5½ minutes to bring the syrup up to approximately 290° to 300°F, 145° to 150°C, or at the stage just before it turns brown.
5. Set on a wet cloth to stop it boiling, or add a small teaspoonful of cold water.
6. As soon as syrup has stopped bubbling, start dipping fruits, holding them by the stems or spearing them with a pair of wooden cocktail sticks.
7. Put each dipped fruit on oiled tray to set. Then place in small paper cases.

Anne Wallace
Stewarton, Ayrshire

PEANUT BUTTER BON-BONS

Makes about 24

25 g/1 oz butter or margarine
100 g/4 oz seedless raisins, chopped
75 to 100 g/3 to 4 oz icing sugar, sieved
100 g/4 oz peanut butter
50 to 75 g/2 to 3 oz plain cooking chocolate broken into pieces

1. Put butter or margarine in a 1 litre/1¾ pint jug. Cook uncovered on full power for 1 minute, or until melted.
2. Add chopped raisins, sugar and peanut butter and mix to a paste.
3. Shape into balls, about the size of a large grape, and leave on foil or waxed paper to harden overnight.
4. Put the chocolate in a 600 ml/1 pint jug. Cook uncovered on full power for 3 to 4 minutes. Stir well at intervals to ensure it is evenly melted.
5. Dip the top of each bon-bon in melted chocolate and, when set, put in paper sweet cases.

Margaret Heywood
Mankinholes, Nr Todmorden,
Lancashire

Joan Tyers' Hints and Tips

A

Almonds, to blanch. 100 g/4 oz almonds to 300 ml/½ pint water. Cover and heat on full power for 3 minutes, or until boiling. Allow to cool in the water and remove skins by rubbing between finger and thumb.

Almonds, to toast—for **trout** and other **savoury garnishes.** Heat 25 g/ 1 oz butter in a 1 litre/1¾ pint bowl or jug for 30 seconds, uncovered. Stir in 100 g/4 oz flaked almonds. Cook, uncovered, on full power for 4 to 5 minutes, stirring twice during cooking.

Almonds, to toast—for **cakes** and **sweet dishes.** Spread 50 g/2 oz flaked almonds on a heat-proof plate. Cook, uncovered, on full power for 6 minutes. Stir after 4 minutes, picking out the ones that are already brown enough.

Apples, baked. Score the skin around centre to avoid pressure building up inside and apple bursting. Core and fill with dried fruit and sugar, or mincemeat. Set in a shallow bowl or serving dish. Cook, uncovered, on full power: 2 to 3 minutes for 1 apple, 1 minute extra for each extra apple. (If using mincemeat, cover with cling film.) Allow to stand for at least 2 minutes. They are too hot to eat at once. The fruit filling cooks first. Test with a cocktail stick. If the apple feels soft in the middle, the rest will cook during standing time.

Apples, stewed. Can be cooked in a roasting bag, which will be quicker than cooking in a dish. Put 450 g/1 lb apples, in slices not chunks, into a roasting bag, sprinkle with sugar. No liquid required. It is not necessary to close the bag. Cook on full power for 5 to 6 minutes. Check from time to time as some apples 'fall' sooner than others. These can be allowed to cool in the bag and then can be frozen.

Apricots, to rehydrate without soaking overnight. Put 225 g/8 oz dried apricots in a dish, cover with water. Cover dish and cook on full power for 4 minutes, then leave to stand for 3 minutes.

Aubergines, to prepare 2 aubergines (total weight 350 g/12 oz) for stuffing, and to prevent flesh from going dark. Wash and dry. Prick skin in several places with a fork and stand them on a plate. Cook, uncovered, on full power for 6 minutes. Let them stand for 2 or 3 minutes. They are now ready to scoop out and fill with ready-cooked, hot filling.

B

Barbecues. Meat (such as steak, burgers, kebabs, etc.) and chicken can be cooked in a microwave for two thirds of the given time, wrapped in foil until required, then finished on the barbecue. Do this while barbecue is heating up. Do not leave partly-cooked food around for any length of time.

Beef. Guide to roasting times if your microwave cooker has variable power settings. Using meat straight from refrigerator, stand joint on a rack or upturned plate in a shallow dish so that it is raised out of its juices. Do not cover. Cook on roast (or 70%) setting:

10 minutes per 450 g/1 lb – well done
9 minutes per 450 g/1 lb – medium
8 minutes per 450 g/1 lb – rare

Turn joint over halfway through cooking and drain juices into a jug for gravy. When cooking time is complete, wrap joint in foil, shiny side inwards, and leave to stand for 15 minutes.
See page 71 for making gravy.

Blanching vegetables for the freezer. For 450 g/1 lb prepared vegetables, put them straight into a freezer bag with 2 tablespoons water and loosely close the neck. Cook on full power for one third of the time recommended for cooking the fresh vegetable. Halfway through, shake the bag to redistribute contents. After full time, open bag, drain water and put bag into iced water to cool. Then freeze.

Bread, to refresh. Wrap it in a clean cotton or linen tea towel. Cook on full power for 15 to 30 seconds, until slightly warm on the surface.

Bread-baking is not a great success in a microwave cooker. However, it is handy for warming flour. The packet may be put into the microwave on full power: 1.5 kg/3½ lb for 1 minute.

Bread dough, to rise. Cover the bowl. Dough made from 450 g/1 lb flour: 15 seconds on full power followed by 5 minutes to rest, repeat two or three times until dough is doubled in size. The same pattern can be used for larger quantities up to 1.3 kg/3 lb of flour. After that the dough may grow too large to fit in the microwave cooker!

Breadcrumbs, dried. Cut 4 or 5 slices of bread into fingers, including crusts. Put them into microwave cooker on a piece of paper towel. Heat on full power for 3 minutes. Leave to cool, crumble and store in a screw-top jar.

Breadcrumbs, toasted. Melt 25 g/1 oz butter in a 1 litre/1¾ pint jug or bowl for 30 seconds on full power. Stir in 75 g/3 oz fresh breadcrumbs until well coated with butter. Cook on full power for 5 minutes, checking and stirring often so that they brown evenly.

Breakfast on a plate. Cover 2 rashers of bacon with paper towel to adsorb fat and moisture. Cut a tomato in half. Break an egg into a cup and pierce yolk with a fork. Stand the cup on the plate with the bacon and tomato and cook, uncovered, on full power for 2 minutes.

Browning dishes. Always pre-heat according to the manufacturer's instructions. Good for steak, chops or sausages – BUT are most effective with small quantities, so it is wise to think of this before buying one. They are not suitable for roasts. Before buying one check that it is approved for use in your own microwave cooker.

Browning of meat joints will occur more readily when they have a natural coating of fat, as this caramellises during cooking. Commercial browning powders can be used, especially for poultry. You may have something in the cupboard already which will be suitable, such as soya sauce, or paprika pepper sprinkled on after brushing with melted butter. Or brush on some runny honey or melted redcurrant jelly.

Buns. When baking, use two paper bun cases in order to provide a stronger container which will help maintain the shape and prevent spreading. *See Chocolate Sponge Sandwich, page 91.*

Butter, to melt straight from refrigerator: 25 g/1 oz full power, uncovered, 35 to 40 seconds; 50 g/2 oz, 45 to 50 seconds. Spitting occurs when it is overheated.

Butter, to soften straight from

refrigerator: 250 g/½ lb defrost (30%) setting, 30 to 40 seconds; full power 10 seconds.

C

Cakes (*See introduction to cakes chapter, page 90*)

When making cakes which usually require the creaming method, put all ingredients together. Mix well, but do not beat hard as too much air causes mixture to expand during cooking and possibly overflow the container. The cake may then collapse when taken from microwave cooker. The right consistency for a microwave cake or pudding mixture: it should drop off the spoon to the count of 3. If necessary, add 2 or 3 tablespoons cold water. Too much liquid produces a heavy result.

Casserole lids which overlap the casserole can be put on slightly sideways to allow steam to escape and prevent rattling.

Casseroled meat. If you have variable power setting the following may be helpful. When converting your own recipes, cheaper cuts like skirt can be used. For 450 g/1 lb meat, cut it into smaller pieces than you might normally. Cook, covered, on simmer (50%) setting without liquid for 15 to 20 minutes. Then add about one third of the normal amount of liquid and the other ingredients and cook, covered, on same setting for 10 minutes more. If by trial and error the meat is still tough, instead of simmer (50%) setting use defrost (30%) setting and add 10 to 15 minutes to the cooking time.

Cauliflower can be cooked whole. Choose one of medium size, cut out the core, stand it up in a deep dish, add 2 tablespoons cold water. Cover and cook on full power for 10 minutes. Let it stand, covered, for 4 minutes before serving.

Cheeses taken straight from the refrigerator to eat will have their full flavour restored if given 10 seconds on full power.

Chocolate, to melt. Always break it up and, while melting on full power, watch carefully. If it is overheated it can go grainy and burn. 100 g/4 oz chocolate takes 1 to 2 minutes on full power.

Christmas Puddings. To cook a 450 g/1 lb pudding, cover loosely with cling film. Cook on full power for 5 minutes. Let it stand, covered for 5 minutes before serving. Under a fresh covering of cling film, fitted when pudding is cold, it will keep for months, but since the cooking time is so dramatically less than the conventional steaming time it is easy to make Christmas puddings whenever you want them.

To reheat a 450 g/1 lb pudding, cover with cling film, cook on full power for 2 minutes. Slices of pudding require only 1 minute to reheat.

Citrus fruits, see J for Juice.

Cleaning the microwave cooker. Wipe oven regularly with a damp, soapy cloth. For congealed fat, bring a small container of water to the boil on full power and the steam will soften it so that it can be cleaned easily.

Cocoa. Use no more than 15 g/½ oz to 100 g/4 oz fat in a cake mixture. Cocoa increases fat content and this can produce a heavy cake.

Coconut, toasted. Spread 50 g/2 oz desiccated coconut in a shallow dish. Cook, uncovered, on full power for 5 minutes. Stir twice during cooking for an even result.

Corn on the cob can be cooked inside its own leafy cover. Wrap in paper towel. Cook on full power: 2 minutes for 1, 4 to 5 minutes for 2, 6 to 7 minutes for 3, 8 to 10 minutes for 4. Then wrap them in foil and leave for 5 minutes. Strip off leaves and silky strands to serve as usual.

Crumble puddings. Use wholewheat flour and/or dark brown sugar for a nice golden topping.

Crumpets, toasted on the ordinary grill, but not buttered until quite cold, may be reheated on a plate or rack and will retain some crispness. On full power: 10 seconds for 1, 15 seconds for 2, 20 seconds for 3, 25 seconds for 4.

Custard powder can be used to improve the colour of cakes or puddings made with white flour. Substitute 15 g/½ oz custard powder for 15 g/½ oz of the flour.

D

Dried fruit, to plump. Just cover with liquid, cover the containers, bring to the boil on full power, then allow to cool.

Drying herbs. Wash and dry. Spread on a piece of paper towel on a tray or on microwave turntable. Put in a cup of water alongside herbs. Heat on full power, checking every 30 seconds and picking out the pieces already dry. When dry, rub between fingers, then store in airtight jars. The cup of water is there as a precaution in case the herbs on their own constitutes a 'no load' message for your microwave cooker.

E

Eggs, to bake. Suitable if you have variable power settings. Break an egg into a cup or ramekin, put it in microwave cooker with a cup of water, cook on roast (70%) setting for 1 minute. The cup of water is there to absorb some of the microwave energy which might otherwise cause the white to pop and the egg to be full of holes.

Eggs, omelette. Put 25 g/1 oz butter in a shallow dish and cook on full power for 30 seconds to melt. Beat 3 eggs lightly with a tiny pinch of salt and some pepper. Pour them into dish, cover with a plate. Cook on full power for 1½ minutes. Stir eggs gently to bring uncooked part from centre to sides. Cook covered for 1½ minutes more. Then uncover and cook ½ to 1 minute more according to taste.

Eggs, scrambled. Beat 2 eggs with 2 tablespoons milk and a little salt and pepper in a small bowl or jug. Add a nut of butter. Cook, uncovered, on full power for 2 minutes, stirring halfway through. Scrambled eggs never stick when cooked by microwave but are easily over-cooked.

F

Fish Fillets, to cook from frozen. Arrange 450 g/1 lb frozen fillets in a shallow dish with the thicker ends to outer edge of dish. Dot with tiny pieces of butter, sprinkle with lemon juice. Cover and cook on full power for 4 to 6 minutes. Whole frozen filleted herrings (2 fish, 450 g/1 lb) full power for 5 minutes; whole filleted frozen mackerel (2 fish, 550 g/1¼ lb) for 6 minutes; whole frozen trout on the bone (450 g/1 lb) for 6 minutes. Remember to cover thin tails with foil, shiny side in, for half the cooking time.

Flour for baking bread. See B for Bread-baking.

Fudge, chocolate topping for cakes. Melt 2 Mars Bars, Marathon bars, or packets of Rolos with 2 tablespoons milk on full power for 1¾ minutes. Stir well, allow to cool slightly before pouring over cake.

G

Gelatine, to dissolve. Put 2 tablespoons water into a cup, pour 15 g/½ oz gelatine (one sachet) on to the surface. Do not stir. Leave it for 2 minutes, then heat on full power for 20 seconds. Stir to dissolve.

H

Herbs, to dry. See D for drying.

Honey. To make crystallised or very firm honey runny again, put jar (without metal lid) into microwave cooker: full power, 1 to 2 minutes.

I

Ice-cream. To loosen in its container and make it easy to serve: 15 seconds on full power.

Icing, Fondant can be softened on defrost (30%) setting, allowing 2 to 3 minutes per ½ kg/1 lb. Leave it in wrapper or covered with clingfilm.

Icing, Royal. If you have variable power settings, lattice work and fine piped designs, which require drying and usually take days, can be dried in the microwave cooker on low or warm

(10%) setting, giving 15 second bursts with 3 minute rests in between.

J

Jacket Potatoes. See P for Potatoes.

Jam, for pouring over sponge puddings, etc. Remove metal lid, put jar of jam into microwave cooker on full power for 1 minute. Jam sets again when cold.

Jelly, to dissolve a packet. Cut into cubes. Put them in a 1 litre/1¾ pint measuring jug or bowl with 150 ml/ ¼ pint cold water. Heat on full power for 1½ minutes, or until dissolved. Stir well. Make up to correct volume with cold water or ice cubes. Jellies can be loosened in the bowl or mould to make them easy to turn out: 15 to 30 seconds on full power – but remember not to put a metal mould in the microwave cooker.

Juice of oranges and lemons will be easier to extract if the whole fruit is warmed for 15 seconds on full power before squeezing.

L

Lamb. Guide to roasting times using meat straight from refrigerator. Stand joint on a rack or upturned plate in a shallow dish so that it does not cook in its own juices. Do not cover. Protect thin ends like leg or shoulder bones with a small piece of foil. Use roast (or 70%) setting: 11 minutes per 450 kg/1 lb. Turn joint over halfway through cooking time, remove foil and drain off juices for gravy. When cooking time is over, immediately wrap joint in foil, shiny side inwards, and let it stand for 15 minutes for cooking to be completed by conduction. For joints over 1.3 kg/3 lb allow to stand 5 minutes longer for every 450 g/1 lb.

Lemon rind can be grated and dried to use later for flavouring cakes etc. Spread it on a plate, no cover, full power for 30 seconds; but watch throughout to see that it does not burn. See J for Juice for a tip about squeezing lemons.

M

Marzipan. To make it pliable for use after storage, put it on a plate, cover with cling film. Use defrost (30%) setting: 1½ minutes for 225 g/8 oz.

Mashed Potato. See P for Potato.

Meringues. Only possible if the microwave cooker has variable power settings, including warm or 10%. A batch of a dozen can be made from 2 egg-whites and 100 g/4 oz sugar. Pipe in small rosettes on to vegetable parchment (Bakewell paper) on the microwave turntable. Cooking is done on warm or low (10%) setting in 15 second bursts, followed by 15 second rests. Repeat 2 or 3 times until meringues are dry. Store in airtight tin. Do not try to hurry the cooking or the sugar will carbonize inside the meringue.

Milk to heat for drinks can be done in the mugs from which they will be drunk.

Mushrooms. Wash and dry. Put in a bowl with a nut of butter. Cover and cook on full power: 3 minutes for 100 g/4 oz.

O

Omelettes: See E for Eggs.

Overcooking dehydrates and dries all food. Far better to undercook, allow food its standing time, then return for more cooking if necessary in 1 to 2 minute bursts.

P

Pancakes, to reheat. Roll them up and arrange on a plate. Full power, 35 seconds for two, 1 minute for four.

Pasta and rice freeze successfully when cooked. To thaw and reheat 450 g/1 lb, cooked weight, put the bag, opened, into microwave cooker on full power for 4 to 5 minutes.

Pastry looks better if you use half wholewheat and half white flour. Not successful to cook the pastry with the filling. It is possible to cook a pastry case blind, then to cook filling inside ready-baked pastry case. An 18 cm/7 inch flan case is the best size for baking blind. Roll out pastry and fit it into flan dish. Prick base and sides, then let it 'relax' in refrigerator for 15 minutes. Cook, uncovered, on full power for 4 minutes.

To reheat a pastry pie: stand it on paper towel on a plate. Do not cover. Heat on full power. Time varies according to shape and size of pie. So, the important thing is to test by feeling underneath the pie, not the top or sides. If the bottom is hot, remove from microwave cooker and let it stand for 2 minutes before serving so that heat of the filling reaches through pastry (and also so that there are no mouths burnt on the filling).

When overheated, pastry goes soft, but as it cools it goes rock hard.

Peaches, to peel. Slit skin or pierce with a fork. Heat on full power: 30 seconds for 1 peach, 1 minute for 2. Skin will peel easily.

Plates, to warm. Hold 4 plates under running cold watertap. Put them all together, wet, into the microwave cooker on full power for 2 minutes. Dry with a tea towel. Serving dishes can be done in the same way.

Pork. Guide to roasting times using meat straight from refrigerator. Note: the crackling will not go really crisp whatever you do. Using roast (or 70%) setting:

Shoulder joints—12 minutes per 450 g/1 lb
Loin or leg—15 minutes per 450 g/1 lb

Set joint on a rack or upturned plate in a shallow dish. Do not cover. Protect bony and thin ends with pieces of foil. Remove foil halfway through cooking and turn joint over. Drain off juices for gravy. When cooking time is complete, wrap joint in foil, shiny side inwards, and leave it to stand for 15 minutes.

If you want to experiment with crackling, cut it off the joint after cooking, before it is wrapped in foil. Salt the crackling well, put it on a plate, do not cover. Cook on full power for 2 minutes – but it still won't be really crisp.

Porridge. For 2 or 3 people. Use a large (2 litre/3½ pint) bowl. Put 3 cups hot water into bowl, heat, uncovered, on full power for 3 to 4 minutes until boiling. Mix in 1 cup quick-porridge oats. Cook, uncovered, on full power for 4 to 5 minutes. Stir halfway through and again at end. Add salt if necessary. Let it stand covered for 2 or 3 minutes before serving as it will be too hot to eat at once.

If reducing quantities for one helping, mix porridge oats and cold water together in a deep porridge bowl. Cover and cook on full power for 3 minutes. Stir halfway through. Let it stand 2 or 3 minutes before eating.

Potatoes-in-their-jackets. Choose medium-sized potatoes. Scrub, then pierce skins in several places. Wrap each one in paper towel. Cook on full power: 5 to 6 minutes for 1 potato. Allow 2 minutes extra for every additional potato.

Potatoes, mashed, reheating on a plate of food is not always successful as microwaves are attracted to the other foods more readily than the potato. It will heat better if it is spread around the plate rather than piled in a mound.

Poultry, to roast. Always protect ends of legs and wings with pieces of foil, shiny-side-in. Stand bird on its breast on a rack or upturned plate in a shallow dish. Do not cover. Use roast (or 70%) setting, allowing 9 minutes per 450 g/1 lb. Turn bird on to its back halfway through cooking time and drain off juices for gravy. At this point browning powder, or a similar substitute (see B for Browning) can be sprinkled over the breast. After cooking time, wrap bird tightly in foil, shiny side inwards, and let it stand for 15 minutes before serving.

Preserves. To heat sugar. Make sure it is dry. Heat on full power. 1 minute may be enough. Stir and heat for 1 minute more.

To warm jars (but note this method does not sterilise them). Fill two-thirds with cold water. Heat on full power until boiling (4 jars will take about 4 minutes). Empty and drain upside down. Jars become so hot they dry very quickly.

Prunes, to plump without soaking overnight. Put 225 g/8 oz prunes in a dish, cover with water, cover dish. Cook on full power for $3\frac{1}{2}$ minutes. Leave to stand for 5 minutes.

R

Re-heating plated meals. Cover. Heat on full power.
1 plate: $3\frac{1}{2}$ minutes; 2 plates: $4\frac{1}{2}$ to 5 minutes. It is best not to stack and reheat more than 2 plates at a time. The plate in the middle often fails to heat as well as the other two.
To reheat a pastry pie see P for Pastry.
Rice (like pasta) can be frozen when cooked. See P for Pasta for a tip about thawing and reheating.
Roasting meats and poultry. To give true taste, always raise meat out of its juices while cooking and drain them off at least once. Use a rack or an upturned plate in a shallow dish. Do not cover. Turn halfway through cooking.

S

Salt toughens and causes dehydration of meat and vegetables cooked by microwave. Always salt afterwards for vegetables or late in cooking for meat.
Shallow dishes are generally best for microwave cooking. Things will cook faster. Round rather than square, oval rather than rectangular. Food in corners tends to over cook.
Smells. If you cannot remove a smell by wiping the cooker with a hot damp cloth and a spot of detergent: put a piece of lemon rind or a dash of lemon juice (bottled variety is suitable) into a small bowl with 300 ml/$\frac{1}{2}$ pint water and let it boil, uncovered, in the microwave cooker on full power for 1 or 2 minutes. Then wipe with a clean tea towel.
Standing time. As a general rule of thumb, allow one third of the cooking time. All foods require it but the denser the food the longer it takes.
Suet and 'steamed' puddings. Always remove cling-film as soon as pudding comes out of microwave cooker. Otherwise it can contract and squash the pudding into a tough ball.
Sweetcorn can be cooked in its leafy jacket. See C for corn-on-the-cob.

T

Teapot. To heat the teapot while kettle is boiling. Run in 3 or 4 tablespoons cold water from the tap, put on the lid. Heat on full power for 2 minutes. Make sure it is not a metal pot.
Thermometers are useful for beginners when cooking meat and poultry as it is interesting to see how the temperature rises during standing time. Be sure to use a microwave meat thermometer if you want to test the temperature while the meat is still in the microwave cooker. Your microwave cooker handbook should give details of temperatures during and after cooking and at the end of standing time.

U

Underestimate and undercook when converting or modifying recipes. Food can always be cooked a little longer after its standing time if necessary. Always do this in 1 to 2 minute bursts to avoid overcooking.

V

Vegetables
For large quantities, roasting bags or 'boil-in-the-bags' can be used, closed loosely with non-metallic ties. Add 2 tablespoons water to each bag. To calculate time for over 450 g/1 lb: for any subsequent 450 g/1 lb allow, on full power, half the time given for the first 450 g/l lb.

Example:
450 g/1 lb brussel sprouts: 8 minutes
675 g/1$\frac{1}{2}$ lb sprouts: 8 + 2 = 10 minutes
900 g/2 lb sprouts: 8 + 4 = 12 minutes

1.3 kg/3 lb sprouts: 8 + 4 + 4 = 16 minutes

Frozen vegetables do not require any added water, need not be thawed first and can usually be cooked in the freezer bag. However, not all manufacturers use bags suitable for the microwave and it is worth reading instructions on bag first. Some of these bags will leave stain from the print on the microwave turntable or tray. For commercial frozen vegetables first slit the bag, then put it on a piece of paper towel for cooking.

Vegetable platter. Two or three fresh vegetables can be cooked together decoratively – e.g., sliced courgettes in centre, surrounded by a ring of finely sliced carrots with an outer ring of cauliflower florets. Weigh the prepared vegetables, arrange them in a shallow round dish with those that take longer to cook in the outer rings. Add 2 tablespoons water. Cover dish. Cook on full power for the time per 450 g/1 lb required by the longer cooking vegetable – e.g., if combined weight of vegetables is 675 g/1½ lb and carrots are the vegetable needing longer time, cook dish as if for 675 g/1½ lb carrots. Allow to stand covered for one third of the cooking time before serving.

Yorkshire Puddings cannot be baked in the microwave cooker, but if you make a large batch one day in the ordinary oven, they can be frozen. To thaw and reheat, set them in a ring on paper towel and cook on full power, 45 seconds for 4 puddings.

INDEX

120

For Your Own Notes, Hints and Tips

For Your Own Notes, Hints and Tips

For Your Own Notes, Hints and Tips

For Your Own Notes, Hints and Tips

For Your Own Notes, Hints and Tips